Open Source Pro: Joomla!

© *Tim Jowers*

Copyright January 2007

Contact: OpenSourcePro@Serviza.Com

Published by LuLu.com, LuLu Press

This publication contains opinions and generalizations and all information should be evaluated by experts. The product and company names used within this publication are subject to trademark, service mark, and copyright restrictions and all are assumed to be trademarked or copyrighted and to be treated as such. Readers should contact the appropriate companies for more complete information regarding trademarks and registrations.

Limited Liability/Disclaimer of Warranty. Caveat emptor. No guarantees or claims of fitness with respect to accuracy or completeness are made by the author, the publisher, or other contributors. No warranty may be extended by salespersons or written sales materials. The strategies and advice contained herein may not be suitable for your situation. You should consult with a professional where appropriate. Neither the author nor publisher shall be liable for any loss of profit or other commercial damages, including but not limited to special, incidental, consequential, or other damages.

Library of Congress Cataloging-in-Publication Data:

Jowers, Tim, 1971-

   Open Source Pro: Joomla!

   ISBN 978-1-4303-0638-2

     1. Computers 2. Information Technology I. Title

Copyright © 2007 by Tim Jowers

ISBN 978-1-4303-0638-2

Published January 2007

Table of Contents

Welcome...8
  By The Numbers...8
  By the Features..8
Executive Summary..9
  Site and Admin...9
    Getting Around in Admin..10
  Joomla!-ology...15
    Items..15
    Article..15
    Sections have Categories..15
    Menus..15
    Blogs, Links, and Tables..16
    Components..17
    Modules and Mambots...17
    Users...18
    Check-in..18
Joolma! Installation..19
  Prerequisites...19
    Apache..19
      Install Apache..19
      Start Apache..20
      Verify Apache is Running..20
    MySQL..20
      Start MySQL..21
      Install MySQL...21
      Verify MySQL is Running...21
    PHP...22
      Install PHP..23
      Configure PHP in Apache...24
  Install Joomla!..25
  Configure Joomla!..26
    Password Pain Alert!..29
    Domain Name How-To...29
    Finish Up..30

User's Guide Link	30
A Fast Website	**32**
Tweak the Global Settings	32
Update the Articles	33
Update the FAQs	34
Update the Web Links	34
Contact Us	34
Remove Unwanted Menu Options	34
Update the Banner	34
Voila!	35
Get Noticed	36
Built-in Joomla! Features	**37**
Banners	37
Google AdSense	38
Flash Banners	38
Contacts	39
Mass Mail	39
Newsfeeds	39
Syndicate	39
Web Links	40
Media Manager	40
Polls	41
Joomla Usage	**42**
Top Ten Tasks	42
Best Practices	42
Security	43
Search Engine Optimization	47
Joomla! Customization	**50**
Front Page Layout	50
Categories and Sections	50
Step by Step	51
Item/Article Images	52
Joomla Design	**52**
Sequence Diagram	52
Joomla! 1.0 Sequence	53
index.php	53

mosMainFrame...53
　Joomla! 1.5 Sequence...55
　　　index.php...55
　　　JSite...55
Data Model...57
Layout..57
Style with CSS...57
Joomla! Security..58
Joomla! API...58

PHP Quick Study...59
PHP Preschool..59
PHP Kindergarten..59
PHP Elementary..61
PHP Middle School...61
For JSP or ASP Programmers..63
PHP Junior High School..63
PHP High School...65
PHP College...68
The Real World: Joomla!..68

Modules...70
Add a Module..70
No PHP Allowed Here...71
Code a Module...71
　Zip It..72
　Publish It...73
　View It..73
　Gotchas...73
　Joomla! 1.5 Example..74
　Legacy Mode..74

AdSense Module (ClickSafe - Special Edition)...76
Google Adsense Revenue Sharing...77

Components..78
Adding a Component...78
Using a Component..79
　Contact Category..79
　Contact Entries...79

- Add to a Menu 79
- Joomla! Forms 81
  - perForms 81
  - Mosforms 84
- Data Analysis 87
  - DBQ, Database Query 87
- Website Statistics 90
  - BSQ Sitestats 91
- Document Management 93
  - DOCMan 93
    - Categories 94
    - Files 94
    - Files to Documents 94
    - Workflow 94
    - Gotcha 95
  - MjazTools Autopopulate For Docman 95
- Shopping Cart 97
  - VirtueMart 97
  - SimpleCaddy for Joomla 98
- Administration 99
  - Joomap 99
  - Community Builder 99
  - Versioning 100
  - LDAP Integration 100
    - LDAP Tools 100
    - Holodeck: LDAP Phonebook 101
- Photo Gallery 102
- Search Engine Friendly Components 104
  - Joomla! Default SEF 104
  - htaccess.txt 105
  - OpenSEF 106
- Discussion Forum 109
  - Joomlaboard Forum Component 109
- Support HelpDesk 111
  - WebAmoeba Ticket System 111
- Coding a Component 113

- Hello Joomla!..113
- Debugging..115
- Hello World...116
  - Step by Step..117
  - Zip It..119
  - Admin Toolbar..119
  - PHP Classes..120
- Securing a Component..122
- TTS Component Example..122
- References...122

Templates..124
- Edit CSS...125
- Edit HTML...125

Final Notes..127
- Moving the Whole Shebang..127
  - Migrate MySQL..127
  - Migrate Joomla! Files...127
- Joomla! Consultants..128

Index..129

Appendix A: How-To Setup a Domain Name in Apache...130

Appendix B: MySQL Database Backups..131

Welcome

Joomla! stands out as one of the most exciting software packages in the world. The fast rate of innovation with Joomla! vaulted it to the forefront of modern software over the last two years. Today Joomla! stands out as the watermark for very rapidly creating very feature-rich websites and for ongoing website additions and maintenance with minimal headaches and work. Being Free and Open Source is one secret to why Joomla! has done so well. Everyone can use it. Everyone can contribute to it. It is a wonderful and very useful software solution and yours for the taking.

By The Numbers

- Joomla! was launched September 2005
- As many as 5 million sites run on Joomla!
- 2.5+ million downloads
- 57,178+ registered forum users
- 150 forum registrations per day
- 1200+ new posts per day
- The core Joomla! team developed Mambo
- 1,265+ projects on forge.joomla.org
- 1,092+ extensions on extensions.joomla.org
- Over 2 TB traffic/month
- Alexa report [October 2006]: Joomla.org at #492 of top 500 busiest websites in the world.

By the Features

- Easy to add a new article to the website
- Easy word processor editor for editing web page content
- Easy menu setup.
- Simple to add a poll, weblinks, newsfeeds, manage banner ads, and manage contact info.
- A complete Content Management System. Simple yet infinitely flexible and customizable.
- Pages are assembled from various pieces effectively like pagelets or portlets.
- Over a thousand components for everything from Document Management, Shopping Cart, Database Query, Statistics, Discussions Forums to Helpdesks and even LDAP.
- Integrated user permissions and access control.
- Standard SQL database backend for easy site maintenance, reporting, and load balancing.
- Written in standard PHP programming language with the full source code provided.

Executive Summary

In this chapter you'll be introduced to how to work Joomla! and learn the terminology needed to be proficient with Joomla!. The most important concept is this:

> The purpose of a Content Management System is to allow pieces of a web page to be manipulated independently.

Each piece of a web page can be manipulated with easy-to-use tools. Joomla! takes the approach of allowing web page content to be made with a nice text editor and allowing these new pieces to be hooked up to menus and as part of a web page. The creation of text content and linking with menus is done in the Administrator area of Joomla!. More complicated pieces of the web page are created and administered with add-in components.

A Content Management System is supposed to be so simple "even your secretary can create a web page"; and Joomla! truly fulfills the mantra; yet, experience shows you have to learn a little to be highly productive with any good tool. Even Joomla! cannot make a dummy productive; but it can make a regular person look like a professional web designer while requiring zero programming skills and zero graphics design skills and can make a technology professional look like a superstar. I cannot help but marvel at Joomla! as I reflect on the web projects I've done over the years because I've seen millions to tens of millions of dollars spent by mid-sized and large companies plus normally two to three years of development with teams of five, twenty, and even forty techies banging away and only to arrive at an end product which could have been made with Joomla!, a handful of down-loadable components, and a small team within several months. We truly are living in an era of software commoditization. Joomla! brings an enormously powerful CMS to the masses.

By the end of this book you'll be an Open Source Pro with Joomla!. I'm sure you'll be enormously productive whether you're looking to get a professional site up within a day or looking for a strategy and an architecture.

Site and Admin

Joomla consists of two major areas: the actual website and the Administration area for the website.

Getting Around in Admin

The Joomla! Administrator area GUI[1] design diverts from the standard in most "windowing" systems because it is a web application and built of web pages. The tricks of working here are to learn to navigate with the menus and to learn that the buttons to save, cancel, and edit are on the upper right. To open the Administrator area enter the web address into your web browser. For example:

http://localhost/bizapps/joomla/administrator/

Login with the user name "admin" and the password you entered or wrote down during installation. Everything done on Joomla! is stored in a database; so you can look there to list user names and can even reset the password[2]. The database underpinnings of Joomla! will be covered more in future chapters.

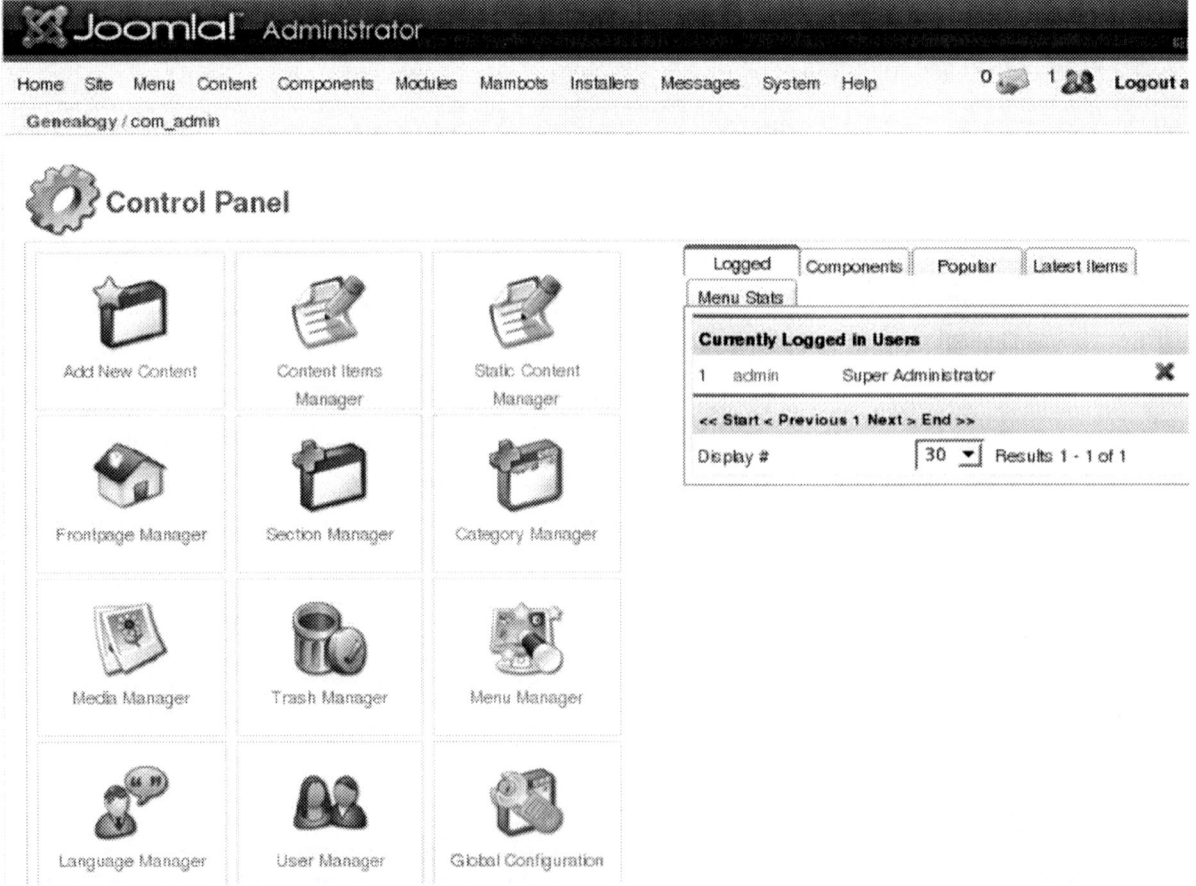

Screenshot of the Joomla Administrator area in Joomla! 1.0.x.

---

1 Graphical User Interface. In Joomla's case this is a series of web pages artfully made to behave like a dialog-based software application.

2 through the MySQL Administrator tool by inputting data in the jos_users table in the MD5 format.

Executive Summary

The menus across the top (Home, Site, Menu, Content, Components, ...) are the main way to navigate. One can also use the big buttons above which are shown on the "Home" of the Administrator area. One can even use the link hierarchy which in the example above displays immediately below the words "Home" and "Site" as "Genealogy/com_admin". This link hierarchy shows where one is in the menu system and allows one to click one of the words to link to another part of the Administrator area.

Joomla! 1.5 is very similar to Joomla! 1.0 but has slight changes such as color, button labels and such. Any example from Joomla! 1.5 in this book will be explicitly identified as such. Because 1.5 has yet to be released, the normal choice for examples is Joomla! 1.0 and most examples are from Joomla! 1.0.11 to be exact. For instance, here is the Administrator area in Joomla! 1.5.

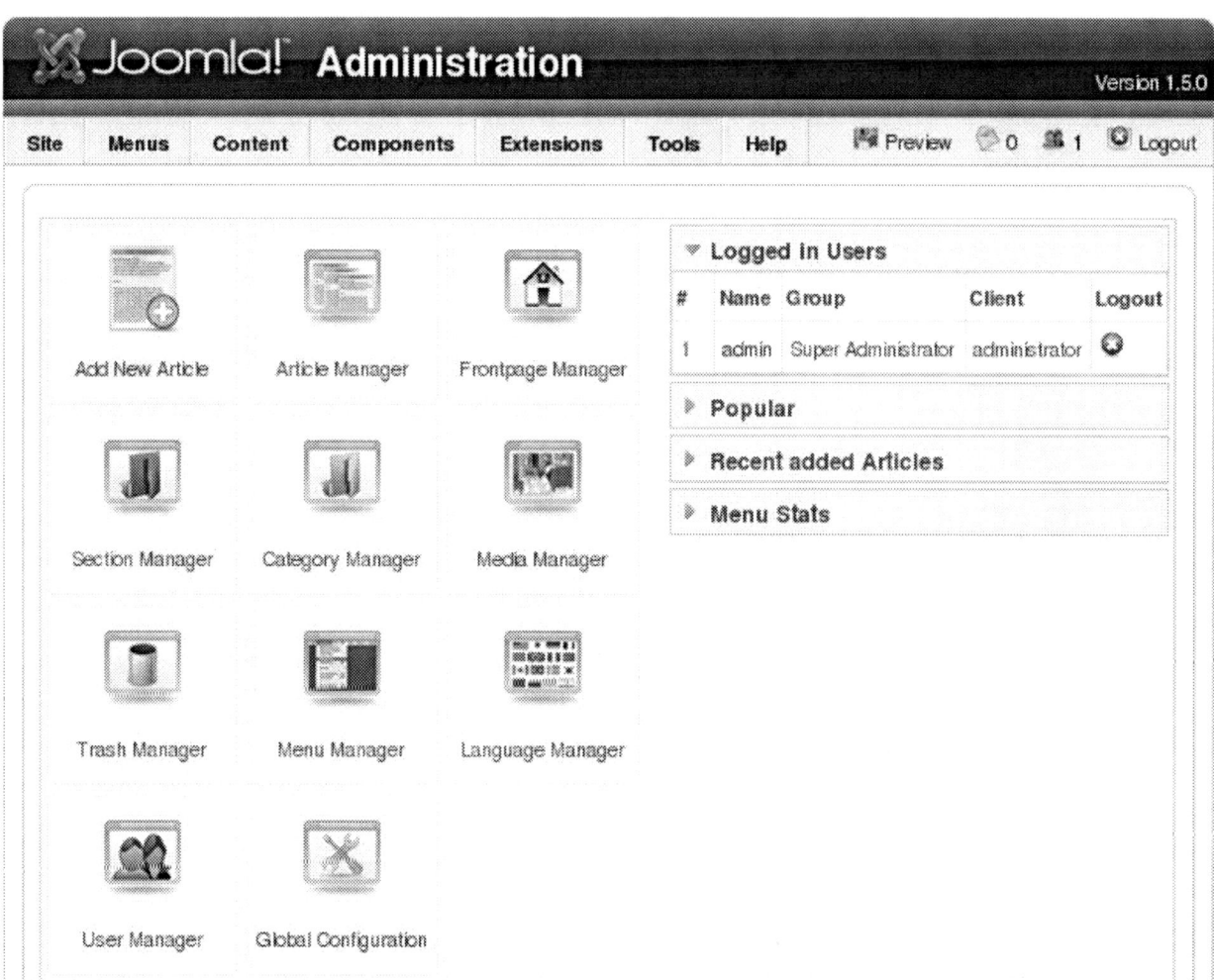

Screenshot of the Joomla Administrator area in Joomla! 1.5.x.

One of the nicest innovations in Joomla! is the ease with which menu navigation may be configured.

Each menu consists of several options, or menu buttons. One may select the Menu Manager from the "Menu" menu in the Administrator area to create a new menu or edit an existing one.

Screenshot of editing Menus in the Administration area in Joomla! 1.0.x.

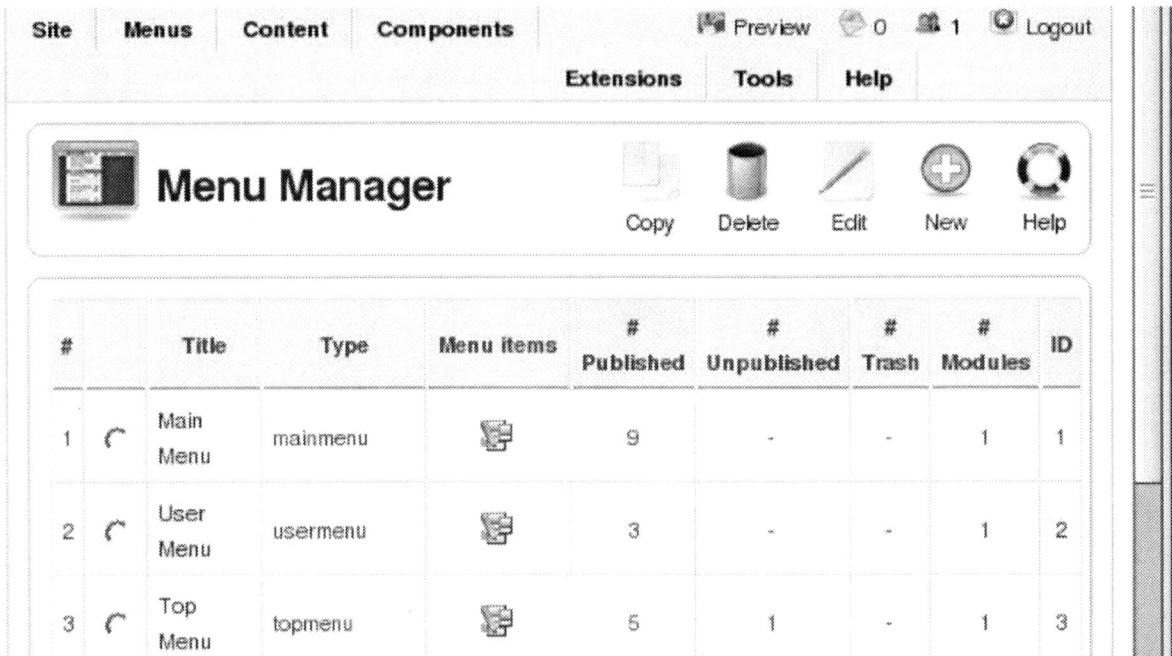

Screenshot of editing Menus in the Administration area in Joomla! 1.5.

Each Component, the Menus, and other parts of Joomla! are edited by selecting them from the menu or from a button as in the prior screenshot of the Home of the Administrator area. The Copy, Delete, Edit, New, and Help buttons are fairly standard no matter what one is doing within the Administrator area. They are the main push-buttons for the Joomla! Administration area. Look to them to setup new instances of a menu, a form, a banner, or add-in component functionality. As an example, consider adding a new article to the website. The standard push-buttons will be available on the upper right as you can see in the following screenshot.

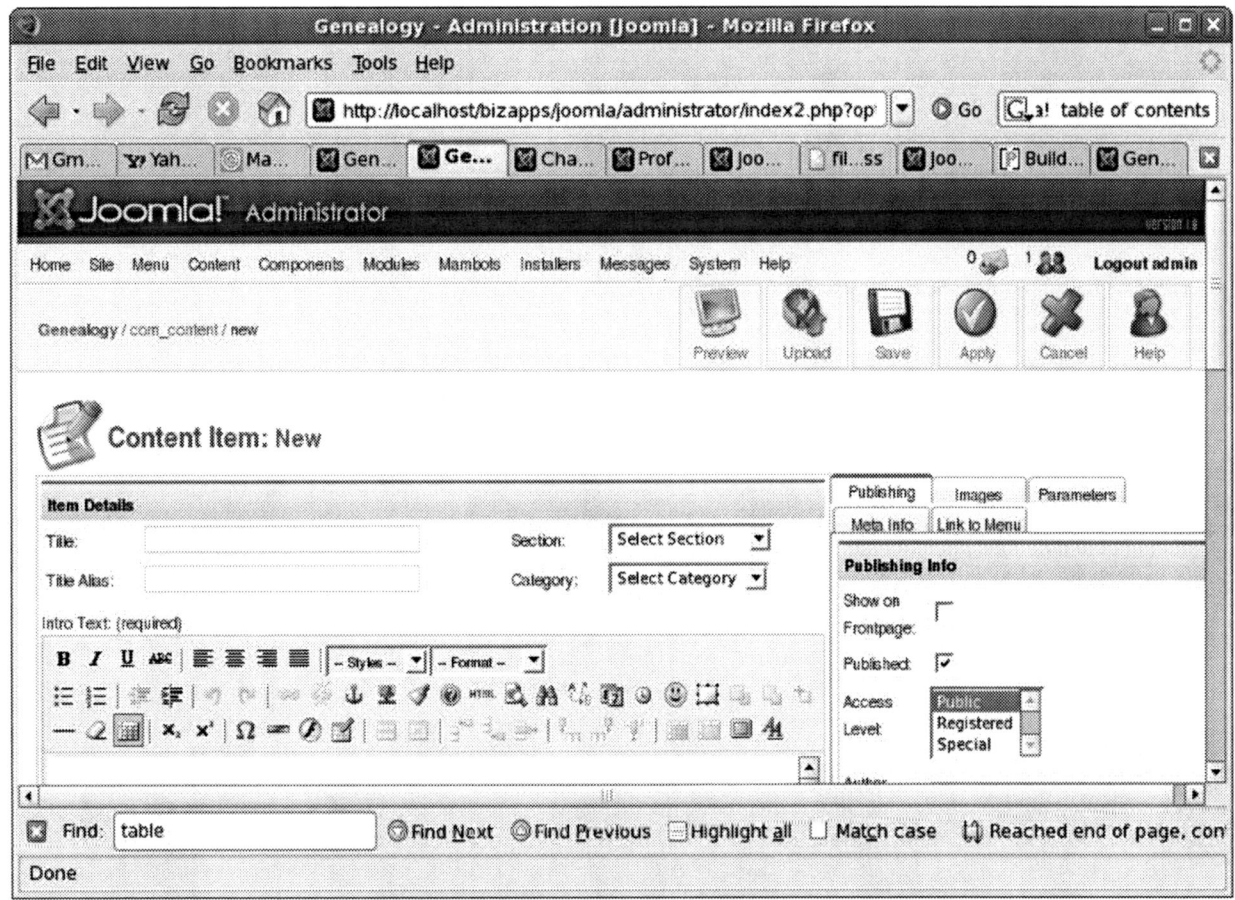

Screenshot of adding a new article to the website.

Each New instance of something has its own custom configuration screen. For instance, the Content Item above is for adding a new article so has ways to edit text to be put on the web page. Each article has a title and may also have an alias to be used within the Administrator area. The text editor has buttons to change fonts, add in HTML links, add in smiley faces, and other common tasks. Finally, one can also edit the raw HTML if one so chooses. On the right one uses the tabs to edit settings for the new article. One can control if the article could appear on the front page and if the article could appear at all if it is published. The article shows up on the website in one of three ways.

1. A listing of articles in its Category may show it.
2. It may appear on the front page if the front page allows enough articles from its category.
3. It may be linked to from a menu otion.

As before, the Preview, Upload, Save, Apply, Cancel, and Help buttons are the main ways to drive the process forward.

Joomla!-ology

Items

The number one term in Joomla! is "items". An item may be thought of as a blurb or article. These may be shown together on a web page. These may be linked from other web pages. And these each have summaries which may be shown and used to link to the full article. The author can embed page breaks in a long article to instruct Joomla! to spread the article across multiple pages and to insert Next and Previous buttons as well as an article index.

Article

Joomla! 1.5 started using the term Article instead of Item. That probably makes more sense.

Sections have Categories

The number two terms are "sections" and "categories". Organizationally, how would you group "items" together? In Joomla! the grouping is called categories. Likewise categories are grouped into sections. This allows one to add a menu option or otherwise select a set of articles (items) simply by specifying the category.

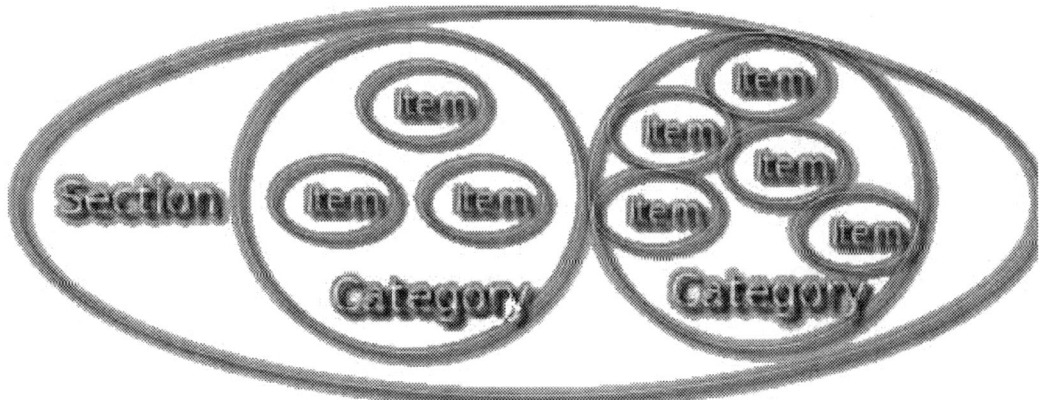

Menus

You know what menus are and in Joomla! they are no different. Links to items and components may be quickly and easily added to a menu. Various menus may be defined for the system. For example, the topmenu, mainmenu (left menu), othermenu (lower left menu), and the usermenu are predefined for the default Joomla! 1.0 installation. The usermenu provides menu options to add and edit articles on the site and appears after a user logs into the website. In Joomla! 1.5 these menus are visually renamed to Main Menu, Other Menu, Top Menu, and User Menu plus two other menus appear in the default installation: Example Pages and Key Concepts.

Blogs, Links, and Tables

In Joomla!-ology a **blog** is a list of items with introductory text and "read more" links. Yes, this is a non-standard use of the term "blog". A **table** is a list of links. The links are all from a commno section. A **link** refers directly to a certain item, or article.

Screenshot of part of a home page of a Joomla! website.

Components

Items are the main "stuff" on the website. Menus enable moving around on the site. Links will be listed to items within sections when a section is added to a web page. The other types of "stuff" are components. Components are mini-features added in to Joomla! to make it more powerful. For instance, the Component menu in the Administrator area of Joomla! lists Banners, Contact, News Feeds, Polls, Syndicate, and Web Links. If other components are added – Joomla! has about 1200 extensions – then they will be listed too. These are not just articles or blurb items but are other content which is generated according to the code implementing the component.

Modules and Mambots

Additional component code may be added into Joomla! as Modules and Mambots. Mambots are for backward compatibility with Mambo and going away in future Joomla! releases. Modules are less complex than Components and used to add simple HTML ouput to a web page.

Screenshot of a Joomla! Homepage showing the page consists of modules for menus, a banner, a newsflash, and a Component.

Users

Joomla! has its own user account system. Users are organized into groups and permissions are assigned to groups. For instance, items can be viewable by public (anyone) or only by registered users. As another example, items may be edited by public or by registered users. Joomla! calls a group an ARO, or Access Request Object[3]. Groups are hierarchical in Joomla!. A Publisher has the most rights of any Registered user and has all the rights of an Editor or Author. Likewise, an Editor has all of the rights of an Author but less rights than a Publisher.

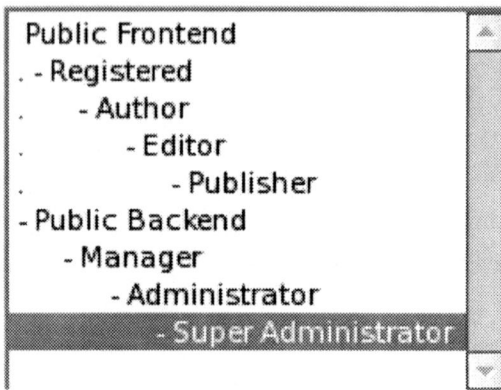

Joomla! user groups.

Check-in

Sometimes an item will appear with a lock beside it. This means someone else is editing this item or you navigated away with a menu selection rather than using the "Cancel" button when editing an item. This problem is inherent in the nature of web browsers (disconnected sessions) and occurs in sharing software from Microsoft, Interwoven, and everyone else. A network connection could disappear or someone could close the web browser program without finishing the editing they were doing. In Joomla! this is easily fixed with the menu option "System->Global Checkin" or by revisiting the item and then clicking the Cancel push-button. Of course "Global Checkin" checks in everything so one would want to ensure no real editing is ongoing by other users.

Example of a locked item. Joomla! believes the item is being edited by someone else.

---

[3] See how to add new groups at http://help.joomla.org/content/view/25/125/
For VIP groups, Gold members, and such see http://www.byostech.com/content/view/8/12/

Joolma! Installation

Installing Joomla! can be easy – if you have all of the prerequisites. This chapter will make sure you are up and running with Joomla! in no time.

Prerequisites

In the true spirit of Open Source, Joomla "Builds on the work of others". The three major packages you will need are the Apache web server, the MySQL database system, and support for PHP. On Windows one can install the XAMPP package or another "AMP" package or can install each of the three packages separately. On Linux one probably already has everything one needs.

Apache

Check to see if Apache is installed: bring up a web browser and enter the web address:

    http://localhost

In an ideal world you'll see a web page such as Apache's default web page. If so, skip ahead, Apache is installed.

Install Apache

Not so fast. Apache could be installed but simply not running. Skip ahead to the **"Start Apache"** heading and try to start it. If it still cannot be found at http://localhost then install it.

The Apache web server may be downloaded from http://httpd.apache.org/. On Windows one downloads an executable and installs it. On Linux one uses the Add/Remove Software tools. For instance on Fedora Core 6 Linux one starts Add/Remove Software and checks "Web Server" in the "Servers" category. One can also search for Apache with apt, synaptic, yum, yumex, pirut or other Linux install tools.

On Linux apache will be installed in /usr/sbin and the configuration files will be in /etc/httpd or /etc/apache2. Check it out with the "whereis httpd" command and by looking at the services using the GUI or "service httpd status" command. On Windows Apache will be probably installed into a folder in c:\Program Files\.

Start Apache

Fire up the Apache web server. It is a program that awaits network connections and incoming requests for web pages. The pages can be HTML files as well as mini-programs such as those used for Joomla! which are written in the PHP programming language. The response from Apache is always HTML so the mini-programs will create HTML.

On Linux use the Services GUI and select the Apache http entry. Then click start. E.g. On Fedora Core 6 one uses the menu System->Administration->Server Settings-Services. One could also start this GUI by hitting Alt-F2 and then entering system-config-services as the command to run. Or use the command line "service httpd start" or "/etc/init.d/apache start". Some administrators also like the apache_ctl program. As with all services, Apache is started from a program in /etc/init.d/. These are usually shell script programs so you are welcomed to open one up with a text editor and check them out.

On Windows one can use the program menu item provided by Apache to start and stop it or can use the Services applet on the Control Panel. One can also use the command "net start Apache" or something of that nature. Use the command "net start" to list the services.

Verify Apache is Running

Ensure Apache is running: bring up a web browser and enter the web address:

http://127.0.0.1 or the address http://localhost as these both refer to the same, local computer.

If Apache is not running then you may need to check the error logs and possibly re-attempt the install. To view the Apache logs on Linux simply watch each line being added to the log file by use of the "tail" command:

```
tail -f /var/log/httpd/error_log
```

This technique is also very useful when debugging Joomla! and other applications which run under Apache. In Windows the log file may be found in the directory where Apache was installed or elsewhere depending on the configuration.

MySQL

Check to see if MySQL is installed: issue the command "mysql" at the command line. If this works then enter the MySQL command "show databases;" at the mysql prompt. Enter ^D (control-D) to quit. If MySQL is not installed then please install it.

Start MySQL

MySQL is also a service and should be started in the similar fashion to how Apache is started. Note on Linux the service is named "mysqld" in keeping with the historical Unix terminology of "daemon" instead of the more in vogue term "service". In Linux one may use a GUI or issue the command:

```
service mysqld start
```

Install MySQL

The installation is very similar to the above for Apache except the MySQL program is available from http://www.mysql.com/

Verify MySQL is Running

One may again issue the command "mysql" and interact with the service – the database system – if it is indeed running. One may also want to run the MySQLAdministrator. It is a very neat program and allows one to interact with the MySQL databases graphically and to see the performance of the overall RDBMS, or Relational DataBase Management System. Install it from the website for Windows:

```
http://www.mysql.com/products/tools/administrator/
```

In Linux one may need to install the package named mysqladmin.

Then one and runs the command:

```
mysql-administrator
```

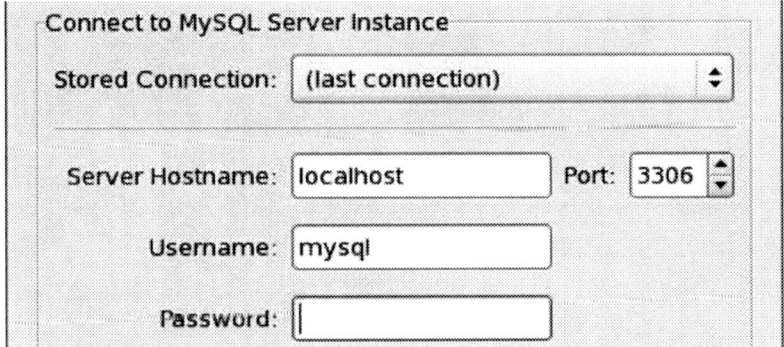

Screenshot of MySQL Administrator connection screen.

For "Server Hostname" one enters localhost for the local computer. Enter the default user "mysql" and leave the password blank. MySQLAdmin may be used to start and stop MySQL, to backup and restore databases, and to monitor the Health of the service and database.

For the curious: one may login with the user name "root" and no password if one is on the local computer (the computer running the MySQL service). Then one can edit the user accounts. Users may be given access only from the local computer or from other computers. MySQL stores the user information in a table named "user" and in a database named – what else - "mysql".

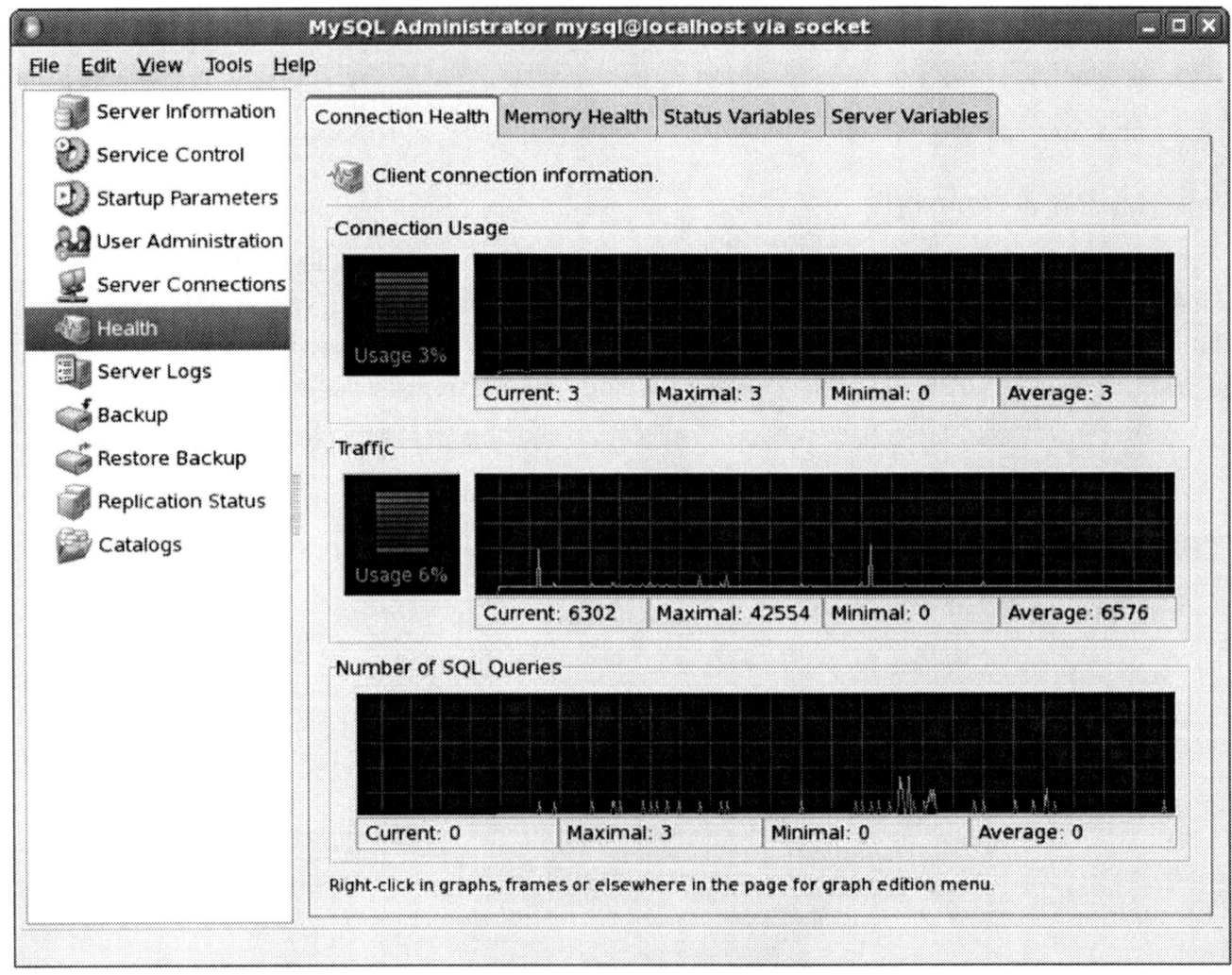

Screenshot of MySQL Administrator.

PHP

Joomla! Is written in the PHP programming language. This language is interpreted from human readable text to machine instructions whenever a web page ending in .php is accessed; so, the PHP

Joolma! Installation

interpreter must be installed. Check to see if PHP is installed. Issue this command on the command line:

```
php -version
```

If a version is displayed then leap forward.

Install PHP

Install the "PHP" package using your installation tools on Linux. On Windows, visit the website for an installation package:

http://www.php.net/

On Linux one will want additional PHP packages as commonly used by PHP web applications such as Joomla! E.g. php, pgp-cli, php-common, php-gd, php-json, php-magickwand, php-manual-en, php-mbstring, php-mysql, php-odbc, php-pdo, php-peci-apc, php-pgsql, and maybe also php-imap, php-ldap, and php-ldapadmin. One may also want phpMyAdmin to be able to administer MySQL from a web page. In Linux one can issue the following command to locate where it is installed:

```
locate phpmyadmin
```

To run phpMyAdmin one needs to do two things. Firstly, edit the file config.inc.php and setup the username and password to access the mysql database. Note this is done in two places. Secondly, enable Apache to see the directory to run the PHP programs there. One way to do this is to edit the Apache configuration. Another is simply to create a symbolic link to the directory. Later versions of Windows include the ability to create symbolic links. In Linux one runs a command like:

```
ln -s /usr/share/phpMyAdmin phpMyAdmin
```

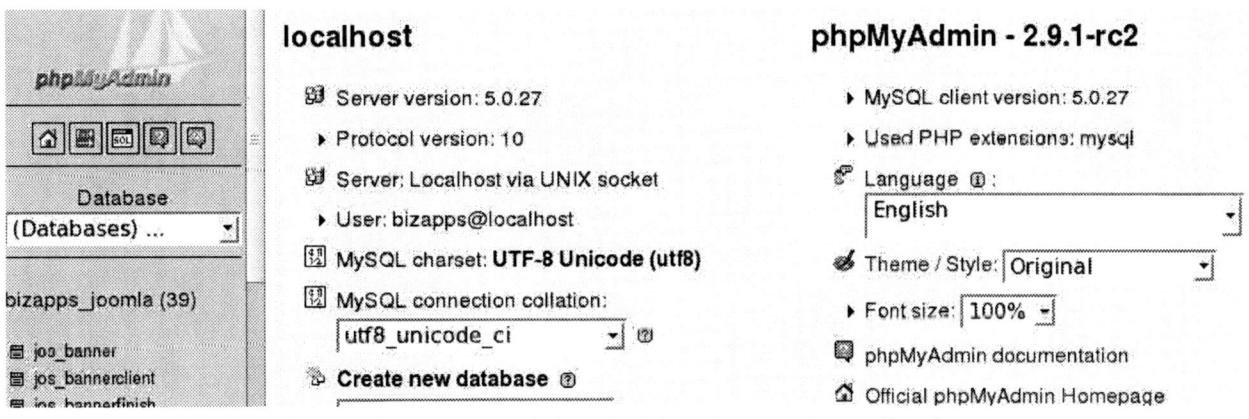

Screenshot of part of the phpMyAdmin web application.

23

Configure PHP in Apache

Apache must be setup to know what PHP is. First of all tell it to look for index.php as the default file to show when one enters a directory in the web browser – just as it does with index.html. Update the DirectoryIndex line in Apache such as:

> DirectoryIndex index.html index.html.var index.php

Apache configuration on Linux is in the /etc/httpd/conf/httpd.conf file, or /etc/apache2 directory. On Windows look in the directory where Apache was installed such as in "c:\Program Files".

Apache needs also to know where the PHP interpreter is. When one requests a web page ending in "php" then the interpreter is used to run the PHP program and produce HTML output for Apache to send back to the web browser. In Linux one can find independent PHP configuration in the conf.d directory in the file:

> /etc/httpd/conf.d/php.conf

Of course the configuration could also be embedded in the apache httpd.conf file and this should be checked for a Windows install. One can review what is in the file to see what Module (an Apache term) will be used to interpret the PHP web pages.

Install Joomla!

Finally we can install Joomla!. First, see if it is already installed. Look in the Apache web directory for the Joomla! files. For instance, look in /var/www/html/ (or /var/www/html/bizapps/ on a pre-configured Linux computer from Serviza) for a subdirectory named Joomla!. Look around and if a subdirectory *joomla* is seen then see if it can be shown in the web browser. Bring up the web page (replace "bizapps/joomla" with your folder as needed):

```
http://localhost/bizapps/joomla/
```

More than one copy of Joomla! can be setup side-by-side so no matter what grab the latest version of Joomla! from the web. Go to the website:

http://www.joomla.org/

Download the latest copy. Visit the download section of Joomla's website and be sure to get the latest. This book primarily uses 1.0.11[4]. The examples are from the package: Joomla_1.0.11-Stable-Full_Package.tar.bz2. The same files are in bz2, zip, and gz formats so choose bz2 since it compresses smaller so wastes less bandwidth.

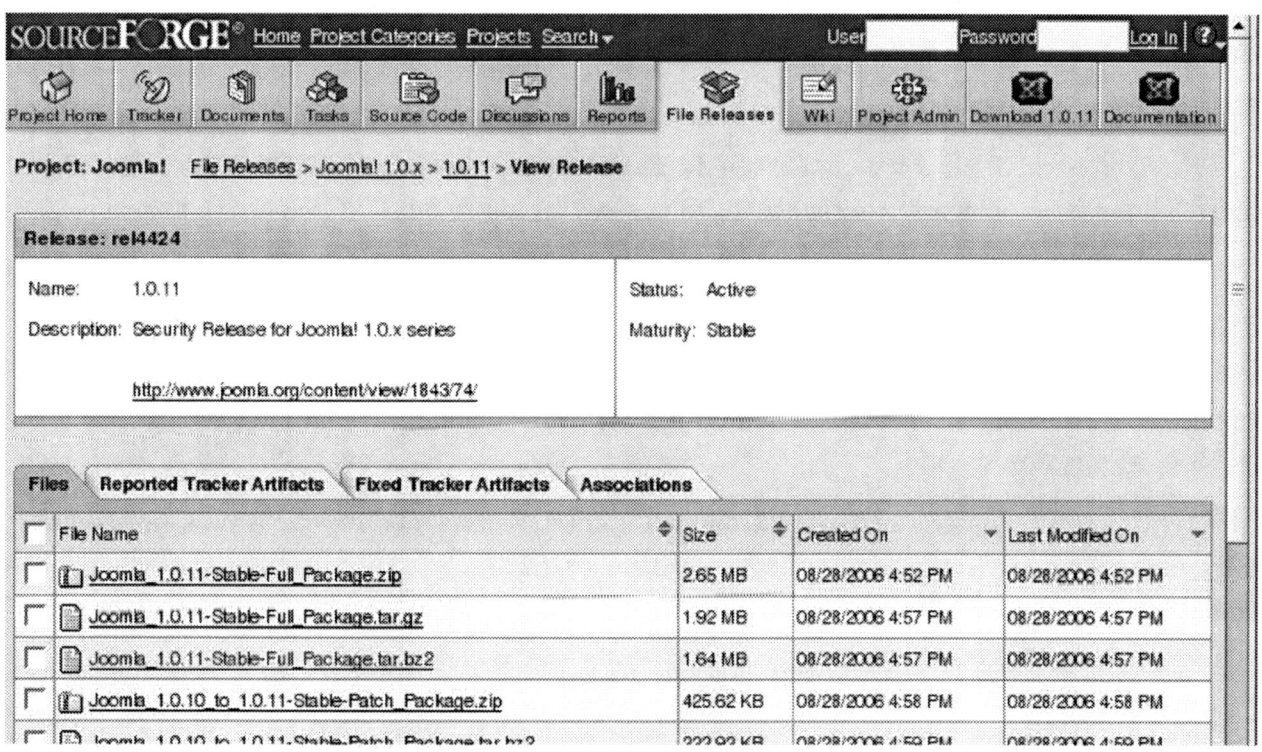

Screenshot of the Joomla! project at Forge.Joomla.org.

---

4 From http://developer.joomla.org/sf/frs/do/viewRelease/projects.joomla/frs.joomla_1_0.1_0_11

Save the file to a directory such as on your desktop. Uncompress the file into the directory where you want it under the webserver. Just open it with the file browser and choose to uncompress it. Be sure to manually create the subdirectory as the default package is not setup to create a "joomla" subdirectory despite this being a standard practice for compressed files. For instance, (where /var/www/html is where Apache looks for web pages) one would navigate to the directory /var/www/html/bizapps and create a new subdirectory named "joomla" and then uncompress the files to:

```
/var/www/html/bizapps/joomla
```

Almost there. Apache by default runs as the user named "apache". The files you just uncompressed will be given another user as their owner. Let's set them up so the Apache service which runs as the user named "apache" can access them fully. One can do this with a file manager by right-clicking on the newly uncompressed folder and changing the permissions. In Windows the file manager is called "Windows Explorer" while in Linux it may be "File Manager/Naultilus" or other file managers such as emel2fm or Krusader. As another option, one could also issue the command:

```
chown apache:apache -R /var/www/html/bizapps/joomla
```

entering the appropriate subdirectory name. As you may intuit, the directory above will be used for examples throughout this book.

Configure Joomla!

We are almost complete. Now simply run the Joomla! setup web pages and fill in the forms. Point your web browser to (remember to change the directory "bizapps/joomla" if you used another):

http://localhost/bizapps/joomla

Joomla! will launch its Installation Wizard. Remember that the host name is localhost for the local computer. The first web page informs you whether or not you have the required configuration. Over thirty possible problems are checked. You may have to install another PHP package such as one for zlib, XML, or MySQL support.

For versions of Joomla! prior to 1.0.11, during the configuration you may see a message about the file configuration.php. Create it and make it writable with the following two commands or other similar commands:

```
touch configuration.php
chmod 777 configuration.php
```

Refresh the web browser screen to see what else needs to be fixed.

Security Check:

Following PHP Server Settings are not optimal for **Security** and it is recommended to change them:

Please check the Official Joomla! Server Security post for more information.

⚠ **PHP register_globals setting is `ON` instead of `OFF`**

⚠ **Joomla! RG_EMULATION setting is `ON` instead of `OFF` in file globals.php**
`ON` by default for compatibility reasons

Recommended Settings Check:

These settings are recommended for PHP in order to ensure full compatibility with Joomla!.

However, Joomla! will still operate if your settings do not quite match the recommended

Directive	Recommended	Actual
Safe Mode:	OFF:	OFF
Display Errors:	ON:	OFF
File Uploads:	ON:	ON
Magic Quotes GPC:	ON:	ON
Magic Quotes Runtime:	OFF:	OFF
Register Globals:	OFF:	ON
Output Buffering:	OFF:	OFF
Session auto start:	OFF:	OFF
Register Globals Emulation:	OFF:	ON

Screenshot of part of the first web page in the Joomla! install.

For instance, perhaps a PHP setting value needs to be setup for Joomla!. Since many PHP applications can run within Apache, each may have certain variables set to the values they require. These variables are set for the directory containing the PHP files. For instance, one may need to set

```
php_value mbstring.language neutral
```

The value may be specified in a .htaccess file, in the httpd.conf file, or in another Apache configuration file if conf files are included into httpd.conf. One can see /etc/httpd/conf.d/ for included configurations files.

For example, the following directive (Apache term) can be added to the end of Apache's httpd.conf file:

>   <Directory /var/www/html/bizapps/joomla>
>   php_value magic_quotes_gpc 1
>   php_value register_globals 0
>   </Directory>

The Apache webserver will have to be restarted after this change. Use the GUI tool or issue a command such as "service httpd restart" or "net stop Apache". Refresh the web page to see what else needs to be fixed (F5 is the shortcut for Refresh in most web browsers. Control-F5 forces a read from the web server rather than possibly from the web browser's cache).

What do you think this error message means? How do you fix it?

"Joomla! RG_EMULATION setting is `ON` instead of `OFF` in file globals.php

`ON` by default for compatibility reasons "

The fix is simple. One can edit the globals.php file in the Joomla! installation directory and change it. Change line 24 to:

>   24   define('RG_EMULATION', 0);

Save the change and refresh the web page in the web browser. The emulation of global variables may be needed for older PHP code. If you install a module or component which requires PHP global variables then you can re-enable RG_EMULATION in the globals.php file or even enable register_globals in the httpd.conf file.

The second install page is the GNU Public License. Good. Click the Next button and proceed to the third install page where the database information must be given to Joomla!. If you have MySQL installed on another computer then you could enter its hostname or internet address; otherwise enter "localhost" for the computer you are using. The username and password should be known for your MySQL relational database. You can create a new user as well. One way to do this is to run the mysql program on the computer running the MySQL database server. Then issue these commands:

>   mysql
>   mysql> GRANT ALL PRIVILEGES ON *.* TO 'bizapps'@'localhost' IDENTIFIED BY 'gr8tpassw0rd' WITH GRANT OPTION;
>   mysql> quit

Then enter the same username and password into the Joomla install screen. I also like to leave checked the option to "Install Sample Data". It is not a lot of stuff, is easy to change, and ramps up the website very fast.

Joolma! Installation

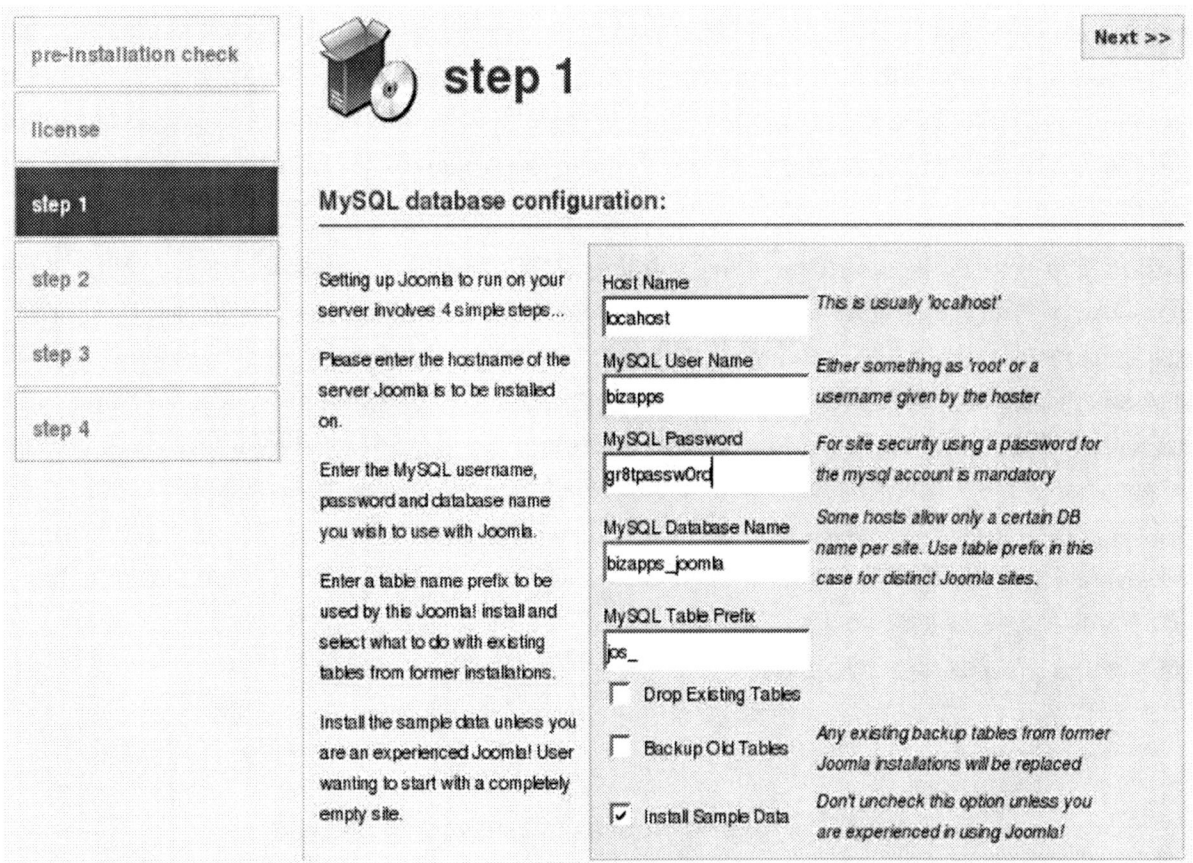

Screenshot of the third screen and first main step in the Joomla! install steps.

Click the Next button and then enter the title of your website. The title will be what is displayed in the title bar at the top of the web browser. Click next again. This next page takes some consideration. How will others connect to your website? Will they use a domain name such as www.GoUno.com? If so then your URL should be something like http://www.gouno.com/bizapps/joomla. For testing and development one can leave the default choice as http://localhost/bizapps/joomla.

Password Pain Alert!

Joomla! generates a password for you. It can be a real pain if you forget to write this down or enter your own password. A real pain starting the install over that is!

Domain Name How-To

Setting up a domain name requires a few steps. The first is to rent a domain name from a "Domain Name Registrar". The second is to setup this domain name in your hosts file. /etc/hosts on Linux and

%windir%/system32/drivers/etc/hosts on Windows. You can do this second step without the first for testing purposes. The host file is an alternative to setting up the domain on a local DNS Server because the operating system looks in the hosts file and then, if the domain is not found there, sends a request to the DNS Server to resolve the internet address. Refer to the Appendix for how to setup a domain in Apache on Linux.

The third step is to let the world know that domain will be handled by your computer. What is your internet address? Run ipconfig in Windows and /sbin/ifconfig in Linux. That internet address, or IP address, must be tied to your domain name[5]. Where? You specify a "DNS Server" when you rent the domain name; so let the DNS server now know the appropriate IP address. Most domain name websites provide a place to enter this information. It takes hours to a day to trickle out to the web as other servers update their temporary caches of domain names-to-IP address mappings. After this, when one types in http://www.gouno.com or whatever your domain is then their web browser will be directed to your Internet address such as 75.177.186.236. As an example, here is a domain name setup page in the Domain Name Registrar mydomain:

DNS Management: GOUNO.COM

gouno.com	A	75.177.186.236	Delete
www.gouno.com	A	75.177.186.236	Delete

Screenshot of configuring a domain name with MyDomain.com.

Finish Up

Click Next and read the last instruction. Delete the install directory with a file browser or the command:

```
rm -fr /var/www/html/bizapps/joomla/installation
```

Click the "View Site" button and see what you have. Fast. And Easy.

User's Guide Link

More information about installing for different operating systems and configurations may be found in the Joomla! User Manual at:

http://help.joomla.org/images/User_manual/user_manual_v1%200%201_10%2021%2006.pdf

---

[5] You likely will want to go to your router's configuration page. The "WAN address" is the IP the rest of the world will need to know. In the router you setup a virtual host/port forwarding for HTTP to go to your computer's IP.

This guide also has laborious detail describing each field on each page in Joomla!. This book, in contrast, addresses the unexpected issues and the steps to get up and running fast. As most of the fields are self-explanatory, this book focuses instead on what is needed to be productive and to customize Joomla! to a perfect fit for your needs.

A Fast Website

In this chapter you'll learn to create your website with Joomla! in less than a day; in fact, probably within a few hours. Simply follow these steps and turn your Joomla! install into a great looking website customized to your purpose.

Tweak the Global Settings

Login to the Administrator area. For example:

http://localhost/bizapps/joomla/administrator/

Open the Global Configuration screen with its button on the Administrator area's Home or with the menu Site->Global Configuration. Change these settings as desired. For instance, the "Site Name" controls what shows in the title bar at the top of the web browser. The favicon is the icon the browser places to the left of the address on the address bar. As well, Firefox shows the favicon on the tab for the web page too. A favicon is tiny – 16x16 pixels – so takes some talent to make something nice looking.

In Global Configuration you will find a Metadata tab in about the middle of the page. Be sure to click it and set the keywords and description for your website. Later you should view the source on your home page and verify these are appearing in the HTML for your web page. View source with the menu "View->Page Source" in Firefox – or the Control-U hotkey.

The Email tab sets up how Joomla! will send email. If you are running on Linux then sendmail is "good 'nuff" in most cases[6]. If not then enter the email server (SMTP server) information to allow Joomla! to send emails.

Check out the other tabs and configure them as desired. For instance, turning on statistics will allow you to see basic information about the people visiting your website: the web browser are they using, the operating system they are running, and their domain. These may be checked with the menu Site->Statistics. Those are also tracked by website statistics software such as AWStats if you have such software already installed. One useful statistic is not as easily checked by website statistics software: what terms are people are using to search within your Joomla! website? Joomla! does track this for you! This listing is seen from "Site->Statistics->Search Text".

---

6 Unfortunately BellSouth does not allow the standard email for home customers. TimeWarner and others do of course. With BellSouth one has to upgrade to a business class of service or run all email through their domain.

Update the Articles

For the second task, rewrite or delete the default news articles and news flashes. These are the actual content of the website; so put in your text instead. In the Administrator area select the menu option "Content->Content By Section->News->News Items". You can check the box beside an entry and click the Trash button to delete it. Notice you could also unpublish it so it is saved in the system but does not show up on the site. You can click the title of an item to edit it. Click the title for the first item and change it. Change all of the text to create a welcome page for your site. The text editors work like a normal word processor. Be sure to click the Save button on the upper right when you are done.

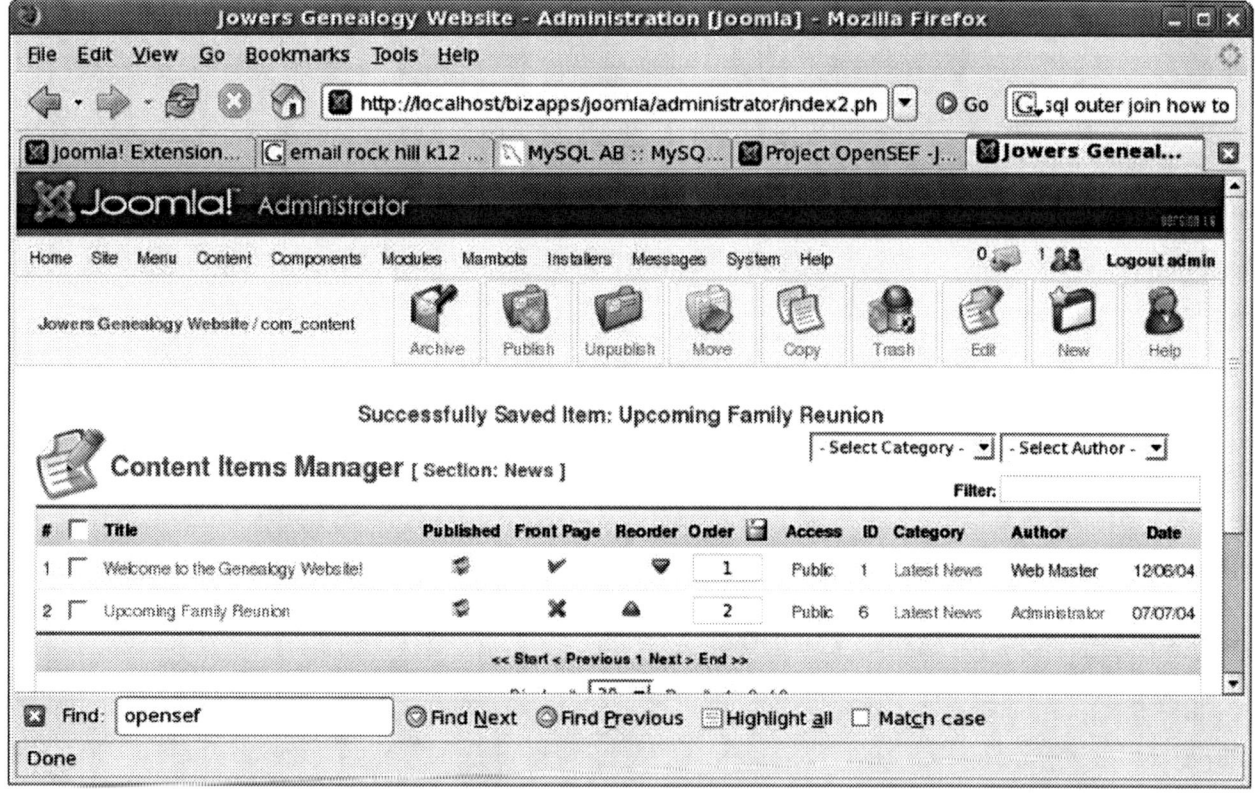

Screenshot of the News Items after a few have been deleted and a few changed.

Repeat the process with the Newsflash items. Use the menu option "Content->Content By Section->Newsflashes->Newsflashes Items". Note that "News" and "Newsflashes" are not an intrinsic part of Joomla!. These are simply Sections created as part of the sample data. You can fully delete the Newsflashes section through the "Content->Section Manager" menu option. Of course you'll first need to remove the Category in that Section and the Items in that Category. Sections have Categories and Categories have Items; and Joomla! does not cascade a delete of the outer grouping to automatically delete the inner grouping. The only difference between News and Newsflashes on our website is Newsflashes will be shorter articles. These shorter articles can appear in the upper right just below the "search..." box and are setup to show two Newsflashes as the bottom of the main page.

Update the FAQs

To update the articles for the Frequently Asked Questions one simply navigates with the menu option "Content->Content By Section->FAQs->FAQ Items". Simply click on each FAQ Item and change the title and other text. Web visitor happiness can greatly be increased with good FAQs. Assisting people immediately with good quality answers is very important although a FAQ may seem like a simple and unimportant task. It is well worth the time invested to make sure questions are answered and fears allayed. Note the many features such as images, authorship, and even click tracking Joomla! gives you even while making administering the FAQ as simple as possible.

Update the Web Links

This is an easy one. Use the Web Links component to update the web links. Select the menu option "Components->Web Links->Web Link Items" and edit the entries. This component is covered in more detail in the Administration chapter.

Contact Us

Edit your contact information with the "Components->Contacts->Manage Contacts" menu option. Enter the appropriate information. This component is covered in more detail in the Administration chapter.

Remove Unwanted Menu Options

Remove the Joomla! License option. You may choose to list your own license information but for this example we are removing this item. First choose "Menu->mainmenu". Check the box beside "Joomla! License" and then click the Unpublish button. Now refresh the home page and note that the menu option is gone. Easy. Remove the Wrapper option in the same way. Unpublish it.

Below the mainmenu is an othermenu with links to Joomla's website and to the Administrator area of the website. We could unpublish the menu options there through "Menu->othermenu" or we could delete the menu altogether through "Menu->Menu Manager". For now, let's just leave it as it is.

Update the Banner

The default Joomla! Banner image looks very good but you want a stylish, customized banner image for your website. In your web browser you can right-click on the banner and see its properties and, specifically, where the file is located. In Firefox first right click and select "View Background Image" and then right click and select Properties. The file is at

http://localhost/bizapps/joomla/templates/rhuk_solarflare_ii/images/header_short.jpg.

Replace this file with your own banner image. The image is 635 pixels by 150 pixels as you can see from the Properties. The Gimp is a good image editor and is Free and Open Source.

Voila!

There you have it. Your website is now complete and ready for viewing. How will others access your website? If it is on a home or business network then they can use your internet address or computer name. To find out your internet address execute /sbin/ifconfig in Linux or ipconfig in Windows. You could also ping your hostname. Suppose your IP address is 192.168.0.32 and your machine name is grok; then the web address to provide to others for them to access your Joomla! website is:

http://192.168.0.32/bizapps/joomla or http://grok/bizapps/joomla

What about people external to your work or home website? These need to use an internet address appropriate for the big Internet. 192.168.* and 10.* addresses are not. Your network administrator should be able to help but the following steps are the basics and appropriate for a home network or small office. First login to the router and see what the WAN IP address is. The Internet is called "WAN", or Wide Area Network, in most routers. That is the address people will use to access your computer. Next the router must be setup to send web requests to your computer. Somewhere in the router will be a setting for "port forwarding" or "virtual servers". Therein one selects HTTP or "80" as the incoming port and also as the port for forwarding. Specify your address such as 192.168.0.32 as the local address for forwarding. Voila, now you can test this out from the big web.

You may also want to to setup a domain name. The process takes a few steps. First, determine your WAN IP address. Note that some DSL and other providers will give you an unchanging IP address (for a fee) while cable and other operators normally give you a changing, or dynamic IP address. The IP address will be mapped to a domain name on a domain name server. Typically, whoever sells you the domain name will also allow you to specify the DNS entry for that domain. For instance, with dyndns or mydomain, one can buy a domain name for about $8.50/month, sign up for domain services bundle for free, and enter the "A" record to map the domain name to their WAN IP address. Then people can use the domain name for accessing the website. Any changes to the IP address for a domain may take 4 hours or more to be propagated throughout the Internet so using a static IP address is preferred. If you have a dynamic IP rather than a static IP then you'll need to update the IP address anytime your router is issued a new WAN address and typically that can be once a month or so.

Get Noticed

Next you must take your website from obscurity to popularity. The most common approaches are to try to game the search engines or else to simply create great content and wait. You'll likely want a mixture of both. Simply visit google and do a search for "submit site" to find a link to add your site to Google. Likewise with Yahoo/Altavista. You may also want to place your web address as part of your email signature so others will see it. And you'll certainly want to visit a few blogs and newsgroups and post helpful responses including your web address. For instance, one blog entry brought me 92 visitors within 2 days of my posting. That's not bad. More information on search Engine Optimization is included in a future chapter.

Built-in Joomla! Features

"Out of the box" Joomla! provides a solid foundation for a complete website. (Does anyone actually install software out of a box anymore? :-) Over 1027 components exist to add in functionality; but look at what all is included with the basic Joomla! install.

Banners

Banner ads have been the staple of web page advertising for over a decade. Joomla! makes this simple. Just add a client who will pay for the banner to be shown and then add the image file and set it up.

1. Add the client with the menu Components->Banners->Manage Clients.
2. Next upload their banner advertisement with the menu Components->Banners->Manage Banners.
   1. The impressions purchased allows an easy way to limit how many times the advertisement shows.
      1. One purchases advertising impressions on blocks of 1000 impressions; so the quoted price is CPM, cost per mille where mille is French for 1,000.
      2. A more modern way of purchasing advertisements is CPC, or cost per click. To affect this one should note this page will display the number of times this ad has been clicked. You can look the new banner listing to see how much to bill the client or can write a SQL script to read it from the database for accounting purposes.
   2. Use the Upload button to upload the image file. Then click F5, or press the browser's refresh button to refresh the listing for the Banner Image Selector. Images may also be uploaded with the Media Manager by selecting it from the Administration Home and then selecting the subfolder icon for banners. Select the image for this client.
   3. Click the Save button.
   4. Notice whether or not the banner is published. You will need to select it and click the Publish button if you did not select Yes for "Show banner" when adding it.
   5. Check the "Impressions Left" column. Entering a number of impressions but also clicking unlimited will use the number entered and ignore the unlimited checkbox.
3. The banner will now randomly show on the web page. The default setup shows it on the front page.
4. The Administrator can look back at "Components->Banners->Manage Banners" and see how

many impressions were made and how many are left.
5. Note. The banner listing magically disappears after all of the impressions are used up. Be sure to record the information somewhere else to be able to reuse it if the client purchases more impressions. Or see the jos_bannerfinish table in the database.

One can also get funky and write some HTML rather than show an image for the banner. Of course Joomla! cannot track what links are clicked within the code; but this is a quick way to ad text advertising.

Google AdSense

The search engine company Google makes its money by selling advertising on the Internet. The advertising takes the form of ads along the right of the screen when you search with Google and in the form of text and links on a web page for participating websites. A company purchases Google AdWords which allow its link to show up when someone types in those search words. For instance, Serviza placed a bid for $1 to show up when someone searches for the phrase "linux computer". Their ad showed up tens of thousands of times. In about 1% of the searches a person would click their ad link. Google only charges for actual clicks so the cost for that click/person was about $0.70. Google also syndicates the advertisement out to websites. It determines what websites are about "linux computers" and sends them the link text to show. The participating websites add Google AdSense code to their web pages. About 0.01% of the time someone clicks one of those links.

To add Google AdSense to your website one can sign up at https://www.google.com/adsense/. Here one chooses the ad layout, the colors, and whether to show categories or just ads. Then one will be presented with the Google AdSense code for one's website. Copy this and paste it into the "Custom banner code" textarea when creating a banner. Voila! When someone clicks the link and goes to Google and the linked website then you will receive some change.

AdSense code can be run without the banner module as well. The code can be pasted right into the template's index.php file. Refer to the chapter on templates for more information about where to find this file.

Best of all, a Module for Joomla! exists to exactly manage Google Adsense code. This is probably the best way to add Google Adsense and is covered in a future chapter specifically about the Google Adsense Module.

Flash Banners

The ability to add "Custom banner code" can be used in other creative ways as well. For instance, one

may wish to have an animated banner such as a Flash file. For this, paste in the HTML related to the Flash module and it will load the Flash file and play it just as is normal for HTML and Flash on a web page. Some components have even been created explicitly to allow Flash banners and better banner management. These may be of interest:
- ArtBanners: http://www.freemambo.com/website/content/view/23/2/
- Flash Banner: http://developer.joomla.org/sf/frs/do/listReleases/projects.flash_banner_accessible/frs.flash_banner_accessible_1_0

Contacts

The contacts component is covered in the introduction to Adding a Component; one more detail bears mentioning here. Firstly, a contact listing may be associated with a user account in Joomla!. This is simply for convenience of managing a user's contact listing. The "contacts" are persons to contact for the company or website and not a list of customers or other contact information as stored with a contact manager software package.

Mass Mail

Mass mail is a simple way to send email to all registered users or select groups of users based on the roles assigned to the users. For instance, an email can be sent to all Authors registered on the system.

Newsfeeds

Would you like to aggregate blurbs from other websites into a page on your website? Maybe you want the news headlines for each day from your favorite news sources. Newsfeeds, or RSS, is the technology to make this happen. You specify the web address of the blurb and the content will be retrieved to show in your web page. RSS is often an acronym for Really Simple Syndication[7].

Syndicate

RSS can be used to aggregate info from other websites onto your website. In reverse, RSS may be used to syndicate info for others to use from your website. You may have daily news such as: the pool

---

[7] RSS for RDF Site Summary means RDF is used so the content is heavily defined and has an exact meaning rather than simply being a blurb. Using RSS and RDF one could update product listings or other higher context data feeds.

temperature, the daily special, or the hourly traffic report. Syndicate these and allow others to show them on their web pages. The News messages from your website will then be available for others to use on their web pages. Modern email clients such as Mozilla Thunderbird also allow RSS feeds to be grouped into a screen; so, your staff could track what is happening in the company with ease. After setting up the Syndication, you will provide the web address for the feed to them. For example:

www.techsingularity.org/index.php?option=com_rss&feed=RSS0.91&no_html=1

When configuring Syndication in the Administrator area, please note the order selection list. You can have the news items ordered in time order, alphabetical order, or otherwise.

Web Links

Web links is simply what it sounds like: a list of web addresses and description of each. These must be grouped into categories so at least one category must be created first with the "Components->Web Links->Web Link Categories" menu. Note when one adds a web link one can control how it is displayed when the link is clicked:

- same web browser window as the website
- a new web browser window
- a new web browser window without the browser nav menus (same as hitting F11)

Media Manager

The Media Manager organizes file uploads. One may also use FTP or another file copy mechanism to put files in the images subdirectory of the Joomla! Directory; but Media Manager can be simpler and useful for users who cannot access the directories directly. Banners go into the banners subfolder. Emotion icons go in the smiles folder. One neat shortcut is on can click the pencil icon beneath the filename beneath any image and the web address will appear in the "Image/Url Code" edit box. This is useful when creating content with embedded images. Best practice, however, is to omit the domain part ("http://localhost" in this case) because domain names do change as businesses rename, rebrand, and merge.

Built-in Joomla! Features

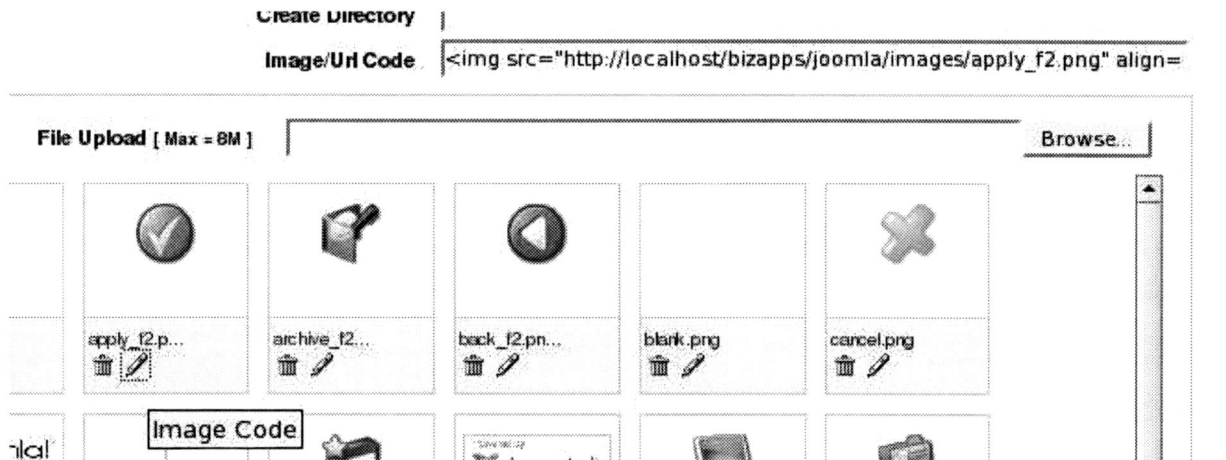

Screenshot of the Joomla! Media Manager

Polls

Quickly and easily add interest and interactivity to your website with polls. List out your questions and a graph of how many chose each choice is displayed for the poll. The web visitor now has, in a small way, become part of your website. Here is a chart from an example poll:

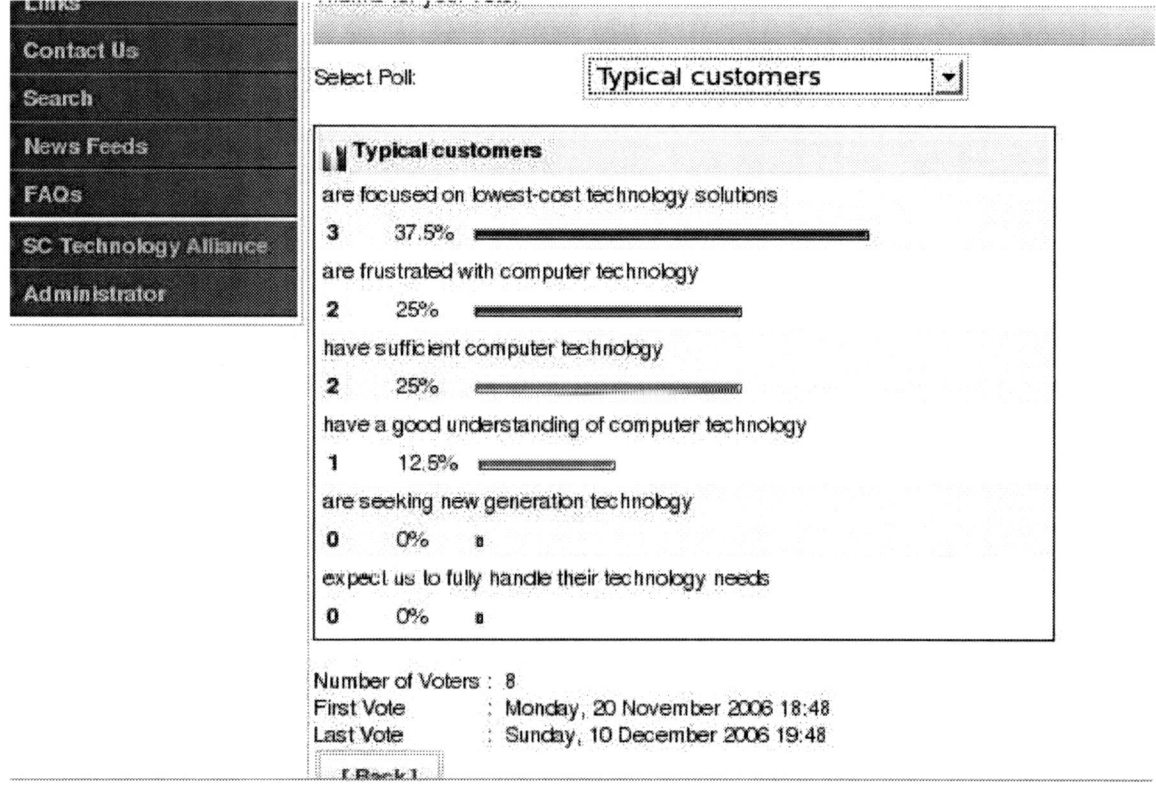

Screenshot of the results of a Poll in Joomla!

41

Joomla Usage

Top Ten Tasks

Summarized from a thread[8] on the Joomla.org discussion forum, here are the top ten tasks often performed with Joomla!.

1. Adjust global configuration options
2. Add a new article
3. Edit an article
4. Upload images and videos
5. Create new Sections and Categories
6. Migrate content into new categories through manual cut and paste
7. Install additional Components
8. Map Content to Menu structure
9. Edit template HTML and CSS.
10. Publish, unpublish, and set article dates.

Best Practices

1. Duplicate your Joomla! Web directory and database so you will have a good testbed for trying out new components and other changes.
    1. One can simpy copy the entire joomla directory such as from one computer to another or from .../bizapps/joomla to .../test/joomla.
    2. One can simply duplicate the database. Use the MySQL Administrator tool or do the following form the command line.
        1. mysqldump bizapps_joomla > backupjoomla.dmp
        2. mysl
        3. mysql> Create database test_joomla;
        4. mysql> quit
        5. mysql test_joomla < buackupjoomla.dmp

---

8   http://forum.joomla.org/index.php?topic=116007.msg582613

3. Then update the /test/joomla website to refer to the new test_joomla database in the Global Configuration screen of the Administrator area.

Security

To secure your house you lock all of the doors and windows; and to secure Joomla! you do the same by locking what any user on the website can to to a certain set of tasks and by taking care to use components which do not have flaws which might give a user a backdoor to access other parts of your system. Here are a few considerations[9]

1. Setup the proper security on the web directory.
    1. The web server runs as a user account on the operating system.
    2. Apache even lets you run as an individual account for your website.
    3. By assigning the account permission ONLY to the directory where Joomla! is installed then you can greatly reduce your risk. The operating system will maintain its security.
    4. Plus, by assigning the account permission ONLY to the database you created for Joomla! then you can greatly reduce the risk of problems with your other databases. MySQL will maintain its security.
2. The Server tab of the Global Configuration allows you to set some security options on the server.
    1. Click Site->Global Configuration. Then click the Server tab.
    2. Note the File and Directory permissions can be restricted to not allow users to write to them. Of course you will need to test your added in components in case they need to write to a directory or file and, if one is found, then you can change only that particular file or directory. Obviously the directories will need to be writable to install new components; so this restriction fits for a production server which is not changing.

---

[9] Thanks also to rliskey: http://forum.joomla.org/index.php/topic,102558.0.html
and to DeafJoomla at http://www.deafjoomla.com/security-tips/security-tips/joomla-security-checklist.html

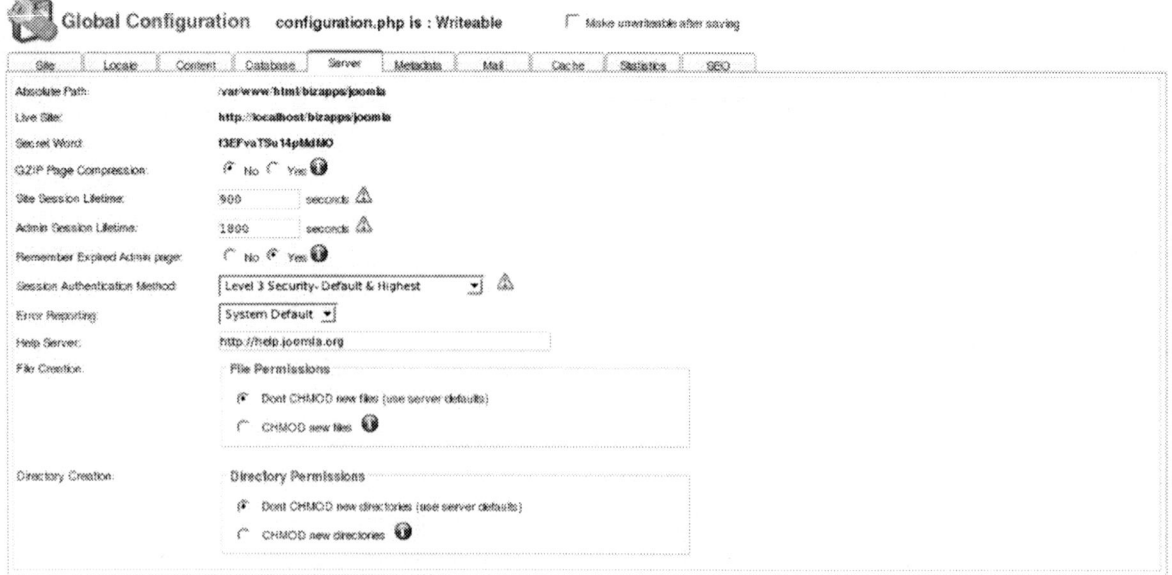

Screenshot of the Security tab of the Joomla! Global Configuration.

3. Setting up Apache user accounts or mapping them to operating system accounts lets you secure the Administrator area even more than the basic Joomla! login. This may be done a a directory-by-directory basis in Apache.
4. Change the user name of the default Administrator from "admin" to something else using the menu "Site->User Manager" and then clicking on Administrator. Don't forget what you chose as the new user name; but, if you do, you can always access the database and read or change the row in the jos_users table.
5. Is your website encrypting the data it exchanges with a web browser? That is, are you using a secure certificate? You can generate a certificate for yourself or rent one from a Certificate Authority and apply this to you whole website or just the joomla directory tree; otherwise, passwords such as the login to the Administrator area go over the wire as plain text and anyone who can access, or "sniff", the wires of a network between the web browser's computer and your website server computer can pick off this data packet and find out your password. It's a fallacy to assume the network outside of your local network is secure. The mafia and others have been known to gain access to networks within large ISP's and even the large telco's.
6. Consider the overall security atmosphere for your server. Is it in a foreign country? Who works for the company? Who can access the server? Who has permission to access your website and files? Who can access your database? What are the controls to prevent physical access to the webserver? If your website is hosted one someone else's computer then this becomes even more important. Who works for the hosting company? Is it a 17 year old teenager who moonlights

selling information to hackers? I've seen that before.
7. Are you doing backups? Better to do them yourself than to need them later!
    1. If you suspect your site was cracked then you can replace it with the backed up files for an immediate, short-term fix.
    2. Backup the database and the web directory.
    3. If needed, backup any directories outside of the webdirectory. For example, a directory may be used by components such as file upload directories used by an image gallery component.
8. Passwords. 9 out of 10 people use the same passwords over and over. Obviously you want to change passwords when you change employees and perhaps change them more regularly in case one becomes compromised.
9. The PHP variable register_globals should be set to OFF. This is done as part of the install. Here is an example of settings for the PHP variables. Set these in php.ini, .htaccess, or the Apache configuration as preferred.

```
register_globals = 0
disable_functions = show_source, system, shell_exec, passthru, exec, phpinfo, popen, proc_open
allow_url_fopen = 0
magic_quotes_gpc = 1
safe_mode = 1
open_basedir = /dir/to/include/change_me/
```

10. Are your components secure?
    1. Test them. Try a few things and see if you can crack them.
    2. Check out the security advisories for Joomla!
        1. Secunia website: http://secunia.com/search/?search=joomla
        2. Joomla! Security Discussion Topic: http://forum.joomla.org/index.php/topic,40046.0.html
11. Review the server logs files. Also remember that each ISP has access logs so a user can be traced back to where he or she entered the Internet.
    1. Unsecured wireless access points reduce the exactness of this practice.
    2. Tor and other IP anonymizers[10] reduce the effectiveness of this practice.
12. For security and performance reasons you may want to test your server.
    1. Run a regression test for each major change. Record a standard set of submissions and responses and validate these work.
    2. Run a negative input test with a tool such as Paros Proxys to ensure the site behaves with invalid inputs. Negative inputs are things such as invalid email addresses, invalid phone numbers, and such to see how the website responds to bad input.

---

10 See, for examples http://www.pcworld.com/article/id,124891-page,1/article.html and http://www.whatismyipaddress.com/links/index.php

3. Run a load test with a tool such as Apache JMeter to ensure the site performs and to find the threshold for the number of users your site could handle. E.g. Your webserver may be able to serve 1000 to 2000 simultaneous users. The bottleneck may not be Apache at all but could be a network connection to a remote database or another such bottleneck.
13. Could someone upload a file named "runme.php" using a component such as an image gallery, document manager, or discussion forum? If so, could they then run that PHP script by entering the web address to it?
    1. Test the components to ensure they do not allow .php files to be uploaded. In fact, check your Apache configuration to see what file extensions are treated as runnable scripts to make sure the component do not allow any such files to be uploaded.
    2. And/or, make sure the components are configured so the files uploaded go into a folder outside of the Apache web directory tree. If they are indeed not within the directories Apache will use for the web addresses then they cannot be run.
    3. As an alternative to directories outside of the webserver tree, one can configure the web directory directive in Apache such that no scripts can be run from certain directories.
14. Consider running an intrusion monitoring and alarm system. You may have an alarm system on your house and probably have one on your car so why not your web server computer?
    1. Snort, TripWire, SAMHAIN are examples.
15. You may also configure Apache mod_security and mod_rewrite filters to block some PHP attacks.
    1. See the htaccess.txt file provided with Joomla!.
    2. See this post: http://forum.joomla.org/index.php/topic,75376.0.html

```
########## Begin - Rewrite rules to block out some common exploits
#
# Block out any script trying to set a mosConfig value through the URL
RewriteCond %{QUERY_STRING} mosConfig_[a-zA-Z_]{1,21}(=|\%3D) [OR]
# Block out any script trying to base64_encode crap to send via URL
RewriteCond %{QUERY_STRING} base64_encode.*\(.*\) [OR]
# Block out any script that includes a <script> tag in URL
RewriteCond %{QUERY_STRING} (\<|%3C).*script.*(\>|%3E) [NC,OR]
# Block out any script trying to set a PHP GLOBALS variable via URL
RewriteCond %{QUERY_STRING} GLOBALS(=|\[|\%[0-9A-Z]{0,2}) [OR]
# Block out any script trying to modify a _REQUEST variable via URL
RewriteCond %{QUERY_STRING} _REQUEST(=|\[|\%[0-9A-Z]{0,2})
# Send all blocked request to homepage with 403 Forbidden error!
RewriteRule ^(.*)$ index.php [F,L]
#
########## End - Rewrite rules to block out some common exploits
```

Search Engine Optimization

It is a fact of life: a lot of people on the website are clogging up the Internet by published web pages loaded with text just to attract search results in hope people will click a Google Ad or other ad to exit their site. Some sites simply copy Wikipedia. Other sites mine the web and copy bits and pieces just to have ads totally surrounding the little bit of text they actually have on the web page. These sites are still very effective and show up high in the search engine results lists. How to they do it? SEO, Search Engine Optimization. The online search results world is competitive so you have to be competitive. Here are some considerations on how to make your website show up higher in the search rankings also called PR for Page Rankings.

1) Do not register with the search engines until you have a good amount of content. This may be more historical than contemporary advise as the search engines will constantly crawl a site if it is ever-changing. I notice Google visits around once a day for my sites.

2) Domain name. Search results factor in if the domain name matches the search phrases. That's why websites like "linux-computer-website.com" come up high in a search for "linux computer".

3) Web page title. The title should match the content of the page; and even a higher search result rank can ensue if the title text also occurs as an anchor within the page. Joomla's basic SEF component updates the title appropriately – see the SEF chapter[11].

4) Link titles. The words used for a link name, or anchor text, figures highly into how search engines rank the page.

5) Keywords must match the text of the page. One technique is to use a keyword density tool on your page and then add the meta tag for keywords with those words. In Joomla! one can set the keywords when one edits an Item. Select the item under "Content->Content by Section->..." and then click the "Meta Info" tab on the right after selecting the item to edit. Type in keywords and description.

6) The site should be easy for a search engine to follow, or crawl. Use of javascript menus, complex Flash menus, dynamically generated links, frames, or links driven by cookies well may leave such content inaccessible by the search engines. For the reason of dynamic content, Joomla's basic SEF at least should be enabled. At the very least, 404 (page not found) and other errors should always direct to a real error page. Error pages are configured in the Apache web server. Sites should also avoid using excessive redirects as many people believe this can negatively affect page ranking.

7) Link internally within your site. A website with a web of internal links ranks higher than a

---

11 Also see: http://www.joomlaya.com/content/view/178/83/1/2/

website full of leaves (pages which do not link to other pages).

8) Incoming external links. Well, this is one of the best-known factors in search engine ranking. The natural way is to have such good content that others link to you. Other ways are to pay for press releases on the web, exchange links with others, blog, and otherwise get your site links out.

   1. Here's the Joomla! location to list your site:

      http://www.joomla.org/component/option,com_submissions/Itemid,55

9) Spend time getting linked from high ranking sites. Google, and probably others, give higher scores to "somebody who knows somebody important" than to links from low-ranking websites.

10) Use the force of Google. Google has all sorts of information about your website and others related to it. Simply run a search for a keyword phrase (word, bi-gram, n-gram) and see what your competitors are doing. What words are they using? How are their ads displaying. You can also use queries in Google to find out more information about a site such as "related:www.kernel.org" to find sites related to www.kernel.org or "links:www.kernel.org" to find sites which link to that site. Unfortunately, Google does not maintain this list for all websites.

11) Do not try to outsmart the search engines. They quickly catch on to tricks like embedding keywords in a tiny font size or in the same color as the background. They employ an algorithm to reduce page rank if the page has the same keywords occurring too often in the page.

12) Submit your site by hand:

   1. http://www.google.com/addurl/?continue=/addurl

   2. http://search.yahoo.com/info/submit.html

   3. Wait a while.

13) Watch the webserver statistics to see what search engines are visiting and if traffic is growing. Nowadays Google's "sandbox" algorithm means newer sites take much longer to gain rank than pre-existing sites; so, add your pages onto an existing site if it makes sense.

14) Whatever happened to DMOZ? Once upon a time someone had a bright idea that humans would actually look at websites and categorize them if they were good. The idea was nice but the humans chosen as editors for DMOZ ended up worse than computers. See this thread: http://thirdsquare.com/dmoz-corruption-122

15) Build a sitemap and submit it to Google, Yahoo, and such. A sitemap[12] is an XML file with your

---

12 Tutorial: http://www.larryweaver.com/blog/2006/11/how-to-build-xml-sitemap-for-google.asp

links and how often the page will be updated.

16) In the end, good content is king.

Joomla! Customization

Front Page Layout

Changing the number of articles on the front page is easy. Click on Menu->mainmenu. Observe the first Menu Item named Home. It is of type "Component – FrontPage". This is what you edit to add more columns of articles or more or fewer articles listed in the summary tables near the top. Click on "Home" to edit it.

Screenshot of some settings for the home page.

This example has increased the number of Intro and Columns so in the bottom center 3 newsflashes will be shown instead of the default 2. The setting of 5 Intro articles will enable a lot more content on the front page. The other Menu Items in the list control the display of other pages.

Next change the number of items listed and linked under Latest News and under Popular. Click on "Modules->Site Modules". Click on the module named Popular. Change the Count to 3 and click save. Repeat for the module named "Latest News". Now refresh the home page and observe fewer links are listed.

Popular can be removed from the home page altogether. Simply click on Popular to edit it. On the right in the listing of Menu Item Links click on "mainmenu | News". "mainmenu | Home" will no longer be highlighted. This removes it from the home page. Click save and refresh the home page. Use the control key while clicking to reselect more than one Menu Item Link.

Categories and Sections

One can also control what articles/items are displayed on the front page by controlling what categories or items are published. For instance, once can open the menu option "Content->Section

Joomla! Customization

Manager" and unpublish Newsflashes to remove all Newsflashes from the home page.

Step by Step

1. Navigate to the Joomla! CMS installed at http://localhost/bizapps/joomla/
2. Joomla! web pages are built from parts on the page. The smallest part is a Content Item and grouped into Categories. Categories are grouped into Sections.
   1. How many Sections are pre-configured?
      1. Go to http://localhost/bizapps/joomla/administrator
      2. Click the big "Section Manager" box on the top right of the big boxes.
      3. Create a new Section for the website content.
         1. Click on the New box near the top on the right beside the Help box.
         2. Enter a Title such as a Department Name or Project Name. For example, "The Monster".
         3. Enter a Section Name such as TheMonsterSection.
         4. Click the Save box on the upper right near where the New box was.
         5. The new Section is show in a list. Note it is Published, or viewable by the world.
   2. Go back and determine how many Categories exist.
      1. Just below the "Home", "Site", ... menus is a link to the website and followed by "/com_sections". Go up a level by clicking that link. Or just click the "Home" menu button.
      2. Click on the "Category Manager" box in the middle left.
      3. Click New on the upper right to add a Category.
      4. Enter a Category such as "Daemons and Services" and other data and then click the Save box on the upper right. It is automatically entered into the only Section, the once just created.
   3. Finally add content to the Section.
      1. Click the Home menu again.
      2. Click the "Add New Content" box on the upper left. Or use the cascading menu: Content->Content by Section->The Monster->The Monster Items.
      3. Select the Section and Category if needed.
      4. Enter a Title and Title Alias much like a topic title or title for a paragraph. Enter a summary and Main Text and try out the toolbar buttons for formatting. Rather than writing HTML markup tags one uses this editor tool.
      5. Click Save on the upper right.
   4. Visit the Joomla! web page and view the new content:

http://localhost/bizapps/joomla/

Item/Article Images

Another popular customization is to edit the images shown with a content item, or article. First upload the images using the Media Manager or another file transfer tool. The default images are mostly 150x110 pixels. Next assign the image to the article. Click "Content->Content by Section->News Items" and then click the article to edit. Click the images tab on the right and then select the image. Note this is done differently in Joomla! 1.5. One way is to insert the tag {image} and another is to click the image button at the lower left to insert an image within the article.

Joomla Design

Sequence Diagram

The following functional sequence diagram shows each web page is generated by several different php files. The overall Joomla! application determines what php files to call based on what components are specified for each web link.

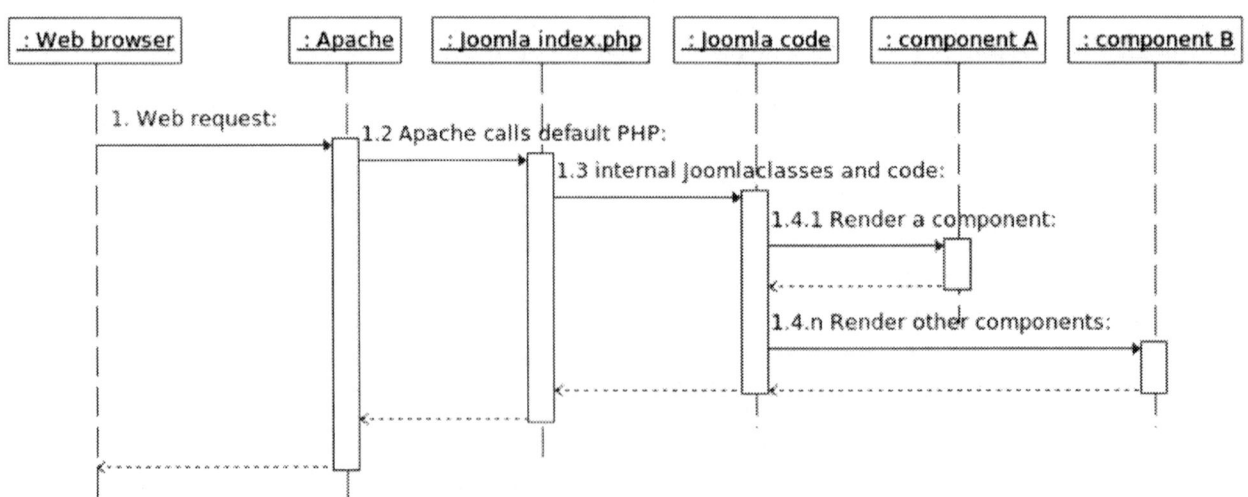

Sequence diagram of a web page request handled by Joomla!.

Consider the following URL to a Joomla! website. One thing is clear, as far as Apache knows, all calls are to the php file called "index.php". The two parameters "option" and "Itemid" are used to determine the php file for the component named "performs" which should also be run. The php file for performs does whatever it does and then generates HTML as output. Finally, the web page is rendered and sent back the web browser.

> http://www.techsingularity.org/index.php?option=com_performs&Itemid=26

Joomla! 1.0 Sequence

index.php

index.php is the main php file for Joomla! and is 257 lines or so long. The code can be thought of as one large function. Near the top some sanity checks are done and then one sees the "option" parameter retrieved for processing:

54     $option = strval(strtolower(mosGetParam($_REQUEST, 'option')));

A little farther down the option is used to load the component and display the appropriate HTML for that component:

99     $mainframe = new mosMainFrame($database, $option, '.');

While the code uses the term "mainframe" do not think HTML Frames are used; instead, a quick View->Page Source reveals a liberal use of HTML Tables and HTML Div tags as are more common in modern website design. In this example Joomla! will eventually call the php implementation file for the specified component, "perForms". The implementation for this component is stored in the file:

/var/www/html/bizapps/joomla/components/com_performs/performs.php

mosMainFrame

The "workhorse" of Joomla is mosMainFrame and is defined in the file:

/var/www/html/bizapps/joomla/includes/joomla.php

In Joomla! 1.5 it is defined in libraries/joomla/common/legacy/classes.php. Joomla! 1.5 is fully backwards compatible but is redesigned to be more robust, have a higher performance, be more secure, and be more flexible.

The mosMainFrame class defines the following methods:

```
function mosMainFrame( &$db, $option, $basePath, $isAdmin=false )
function getClientID( $client )
function getClientName( $client_id )
function getBasePath( $client=0, $addTrailingSlash=true )
function setPageTitle( $title=null )
function addMetaTag( $name, $content, $prepend='', $append='' )
function appendMetaTag( $name, $content )
function prependMetaTag( $name, $content )
function addCustomHeadTag( $html )
function getHead()
function getPageTitle()
function getCustomPathWay()
function getUserState( $var_name )
function getUserStateFromRequest( $var_name, $req_name, $var_default=null )
function setUserState( $var_name, $var_value )
function initSession()
function initSessionAdmin($option, $task)
function setSessionGarbageClean()
function sessionCookieName()
function sessionCookieValue( $id=null )
function remCookieName_User()
function remCookieName_Pass()
function remCookieValue_User( $username )
function remCookieValue_Pass( $passwd )
function login( $username=null,$passwd=null, $remember=0, $userid=NULL )
function logout()
function getUser()
function getCfg( $varname )
function _setTemplate( $isAdmin=false )
function _setAdminPaths( $option, $basePath='.' )
function getPath( $varname, $option='' )
function detect()
function getItemid( $id, $typed=1, $link=1, $bs=1, $bc=1, $gbs=1 )
function getBlogSectionCount( )
function getBlogCategoryCount( )
function getGlobalBlogSectionCount( )
function getStaticContentCount( )
function getContentItemLinkCount( )
function set( $property, $value=null )
function get($property, $default=null)
function isAdmin()
```

That's alot of functions. These cover database queries to read configured data, user authentication, preparing the web page, plus several other utility functions.

Joomla! 1.5 Sequence

Just like Joomla! 1.0 the web address for pages contains components and other request parameters.

http://localhost/bizapps/joomla15/index.php?option=com_content&task=view&id=25&Itemid=

index.php

Index.php receives the request from Apache and then uses the JSite class to call the appropriate components.

    25     $mainframe = new JSite();

Index.php now contains some preprocessing and post-processing functionality with the onBeforeStart, onAfterStart, onBeforeDisplay, and onAfterDisplay events. As in Joomla! 1.0 the $mainframe object processes the web request.

    71     $mainframe->execute($option);

JSite

In Joomla! 1.5, $mainframe is an instance of the JSite class. The same variable name, $mainframe, is used but rather than being a mosMainFrame as in Joomla! 1.0 it is a JSite object. JSite is defined in the file includes/application.php. JSite is a subclass of JApplication meaning it is everything a JApplication is plus has additional functionality. JApplication is defined in the file libraries/joomla/application/application.php.

Below is the class hierarchy for Joomla! 1.5. The items at the top with a # are attributes (data). The items with a + are public functions accessible by any other code in the interpreter. The items underlined are static class functions meaning only one function exists for the entire interpreter rather than a separate function for each instance of a class. Note that the static function does not overlap with multiple copies of Joomla! on the same machine because of how the files defining the classes are distinct. The functions with a # have protected access. This nomenclature is defined by UML, the Unified Modeling Language, and is the standard for diagramming computer programs.

Joomla Design

JObject
- + JObject()
- + __construct()
- + set($property : string, $value : string)
- + get($property : string, $value : string)
- + getPublicProperties()
- + toString()

JApplication
- # $_pathway : string
- # $_clientId : string
- # $_baseURL : string
- # $_messageQueue : array
- + execute($option :)
- + redirect($url : string, $message : string = '', $msg_type : string = message)
- + enqueueMessage($msg : string, $type : string = message)
- + getMessageQueue()
- + getCfg($varname : string)
- + getUserState($key : string)
- + setUserState($key : string, $value : string)
- + getUserStateFromRequest($key : string, $request : string, $default : string = null)
- + registerEvent($event : string, $handler : string)
- + triggerEvent($event : string, $args : string)
- + login($username : string, $password : string)
- + logout()
- + setSession($name : string)
- + setLanguage($lang : string)
- + setConfiguration($file : string, $type : string = config)
- + getTemplate()
- + getPathWay()
- - _createPathWay()
- - _createConfiguration($file : , $type : string = PHP)
- - _createSession($name : string)
- + getClientId()
- + isAdmin()
- + isSite()

JSite
- + authorize($itemid : int)
- + setPageTitle($title : string = null)
- + getPageTitle()
- + setLegacy($force : bool = false)
- # _display()

Class Diagram of Joomla! 1.5

Data Model

One can easily list the tables in the Joomla! database with various graphical tools such as SQuirreL and MySQL Administrator or with the mysql command "show tables;". The Joomla! 1.5 data model has been well documented by Torkil Johnsen on his website

http://www.bedre.no/joomla_tutorials/for_utviklere/joomla_1.5_database_schema.html

He reverse engineered the model from the database in MySQL and manually updated the relationships. He used DBDesigner from http://fabforce.net/dbdesigner4/.

Layout

Joomla! layouts make use of keywords like "left" and "right" known as "Semantic Markup"; so, to create or edit a template one edits the index.php for the layout. Consider the default template:

```
/bizapps/joomla/templates/rhuk_so/index.php
```

Within this template one can see where the modules to be displayed along the left are loaded:

```
54    <?php mosLoadModules ( 'left', -2 ); ?>
```

Use the menu option "Site->Preview->Inline with Positions" to see a nifty view of your website complete with the positions identified for modules. This view allows you to determine where a label such as "left" will position a module. Refer to Compass Design for a tutorial[13] on making ones' own template. Or refer to the online Joomla! documentation at:
http://help.joomla.org/content/category/12/115/125/.

Style with CSS

The Joomla! Template also defines the style to be used on the website. For instance, one may want to change the style to reflect company colors and standards. Edit the default to customize the styles to your website or refer to it as an example:

```
/bizapps/joomla/templates/rhuk_solarflare_ii/css/template_css.css
```

In the templates directory one finds the layout, style sheet, and images. The directory structure is:

```
/templates
  /template_name
    index.php
    template_thumbnail.png
    templateDetails.xml
    /css
      template_css.css
    /images
```

Refer to the Templates chapter for more info.

---

[13] http://www.compassdesigns.net/tutorials/joomla-tutorials/installing-joomla-doctype-and-the-blank-joomla-template.html

Joomla! Security

Joomla! uses groups and actions as the primitives in its security model. A group is called an Access Request Object, or ARO. An action can be reading an article, editing a document, logging in, or entering a form. An action is called an Access Control Object, or ACO. Refer to includes/gacl_api.class.php and includes/gacl.class.php for implementation details and for functions usable in your Component or Module. Refer to the GACL website for more information:

http://phpgacl.sourceforge.net/

Joomla! API

Joomla! provides a set of built-in functions for authors of Components and other code to use. Above is the security API, GACL. Additional functions may be found throughout the includes directory. You will probably notice the "@" annotations in the comments. Joomla! leverages PHPDocumenter to generate readable documentation for the functions and classes. This documentation also has cross references to other files. This is equivalent to JavaDoc in for the Java programming language. Here are some of the functions available in Joomla! programming.

- mosCountModules
- mosGetParam
- mosHTML class
- mosHTML::BackButton
- mosHTML::CloseButton
- mosHTML::emailCloaking
- mosHTML::idBox
- mosHTML::integerSelectList
- mosHTML::makeOption
- mosHTML::monthSelectList
- mosHTML::PrintIcon
- mosHTML::radioList
- mosHTML::selectList
- mosHTML::sortIcon
- mosHTML::treeSelectList
- mosHTML::yesnoRadioList
- mosHTML::yesnoSelectList
- mosLoadComponent
- mosLoadModules
- mosMainBody
- mosObjectToArray
- mosToolTip

For Joomla! 1.5 refer to the online documentation at
http://help.joomla.org/content/category/12/108/125/.

For the latest stable release of Joomla! refer to the online PHPDocumenter output at:
http://help.joomla.org/api/

PHP Quick Study

You may or may not be a programmer already. Either way, you can work with Joomla! code by making small changes and testing the changes. Review the Apache error_log along the way. And always keep unchanged backup copies of files you are changing. As with any language, you have to learn to read before you can write. Read through the code for a Component or Module. Read through index.php. These files all have the source PHP code so you are welcomed to read and learn. The rest of the next few pages will summarize PHP in a no-nonsense fashion. Feel free to use other references for more information. For example:

- Zend's introduction to PHP: http://devzone.zend.com/manual/view/page/introduction.html
- Codewalker's PHP How-To Tutorials: http://codewalkers.com/tutorials.php?c=5

PHP Preschool

In preschool a child learns the ABC's. In PHP likewise one must realize certain keywords trigger the interpreter to do different things.

print()	echo()	return()	exit()	die()	array()	eval	true, false
if	else	elseif	endif	list()	empty()	isset()	unset()
switch	case	default	break	endswitch	abstract	clone	this
while	endwhile	for	endfor	do	foreach	endforeach	continue
and	or	xor	__FILE__	__LINE__	__FUNCTION__	__CLASS__	__METHOD__
as	null	require()	require_once()	include_once()	include()	use	php_user_filter
var	function	cfunction	old_function	static	global	const	final
declare	enddeclare	new	class	extends	exception	interface	implements
try	catch	throw	public	private	protected	self	parent

In PHP one stores a temporary value in a variable. Variable names start with $. Go figure.

PHP Kindergarten

You can guess what most of the keywords do. They are the same ideas as any other programming language. For example, the "if" conditional says to either do one thing or another.

```
<?
$tempNi = 450;
$degrees = "degrees";
```

```
if( $temp > 575 )
{ echo 'non-magnetic. Past Curie Temperature.'; }
else
{ echo "The temperature is " . $tempNi . " and must rise " . (575 -
$tempNi) . " more $degrees";
}
?>
```

The code above shows how PHP works. $ must be used to name variables. Variables are dynamically set to be a number such as 450 or a string of characters such as "degrees". It wouldn't make sense to write ($degrees - $tempNi) but because the variables are dynamically set this could be done. The "result" would be -450 but is obviously meaningless.

The if statement above does not make use of the ifend keyword. It can be added after the last } but is optional. One could remove the { and } marks altogether and use ifend. This would make PHP similar to Visual Basic or some shell scripting languages. Using the { and } is more the style of C/C++ and Java. PHP allows either. PHP includes a large amount of C-like syntax as does PERL which contributed to the birth of PHP.

The echo keyword tells PHP to write out the string after the word "echo". If the program is run in a terminal/command shell then it will write out to the screen. If the program is part of a web page then it will write back as part of the web page HTML output. Note the use of . to concatenate strings together. The same concatenation performance issue common in other languages occurs in PHP: concatenating 6 strings together will be slower than writing one large string. Also, echo and print keywords do about the same thing except print returns a result value; so, some programmers prefer echo for imperceptibly perkier performance over print – the performance difference will not be even close to perceivable. Notice how the variable $tempNi is concatenated with the . but the variable $degrees appears as part of the string in quotes. Variable substitution into strings is done in shell scripting languages so no surprise here as PHP grew out of Perl. Put a \ before the $degrees to print the word "$degrees"; but what happens when the code has $$degrees? Try it and see.

PHP can be run from the command line. Enter the code above into a file and execute:
```
php -f filename.php
```
PHP can also be run from a web page. Copy the file to:
/var/www/html/ or wherever the Apache directory is for your webserver installation.

Bring up the web page to it. Notice the file should end in "php" as that is what Apache is configured to handle as a PHP script. Apache passes it off to a PHP interpreter. E.g.
```
http://localhost/filename.php
```
Of course the HTML returned to the web browser is not really valid HTML as it is missing HTML tags. A lot of HTML tags could be added. That would, of course, make the program a lot longer.

PHP Elementary

PHP first and foremost is used to make web pages. I've never actually heard of it being used outside of Apache for anything real. Anyone?

The top thing for a web page is to submit a web page form. Here, in all of its glory, is a web page form with PHP code to respond to the input. The file is named someother.php.

```
<html>
<head><title>PHP is fast and easy</title></head>
<body>
<form action="someother.php" method="post">
Enter an adjective: <input type="text" name="msg" size="30">
<br>
<input type="submit" value="Add">
</form>
<?php
$input = $_POST['msg'];
// use it
echo "Your adjective is: <i>$input</i>";
?>
</body>
</html>
```

PHP code is delineated with <? and ?>. <?php may also be used as a longer form of <?. This serves the identical purpose to <% in JSP or ASP – to separate code from regular HTML. The PHP interpreter picks out the code as anything between <? and ?> and runs the program. Then any print or echo output is merged into the HTML and sent to Apache and then to the web browser. Web browsers communicate with web servers like Apache by sending over Request parameters and Cookie values. Request parameters are HTML form fields or anything after a ? in the URL. Cookies are stored in a file on the person's computer and the cookies assigned to a website (by a domain name match) are passed along with each web request. In this case, the HTML <form> specifies the action type will be to POST the data. This means the data will be in the $_POST array of PHP. The PHP Apache module (the interpreter) knows how to retrieve the data from Apache from the HTTP packet and creates an array in which to store the data. The array associates words with entries and is sometimes called a dictionary or a map. The word 'msg' helps reference the actual value passed from the web browser became that is the "name" given to the form's input field.

PHP Middle School

Now let's step it up a notch. Let's write a real and useful web app. This will be a story concocter in the spirit of Mad Libs. Store the story in an array. Receive adjectives and nouns from the web page and put them into the story. Then display the story. Here we go:

```
<html>
<head><title>PHP is fast and easy</title></head>
<body>
<form action="file3.php" method="post">
<br><br>
Enter an adjective: <input type="text" name="msg" size="30">
<br>
<input type="submit" name="subtype" value="Add">
<input type="submit" name="subtype" value="Restart">
</form>
<?

$input = $_POST['msg'];
$submit_type = $_POST['subtype'];

if( $submit_type == "Add" )
  $story = array(0 => "It was the ", 2 => " of times. It was the ", 4 => " of times. ", 7 => " very ", 9 => " about it." );
  $story["thanks"] = " Thank you for your words! ";
?>
 <br><center>
<?
  foreach( $story as $words ) {
     echo $words;
     echo $input;
  }

  echo "<br></center>";
ifend

?>
</body>
</html>
```

This file is named "file3.php" as one may guess from the action for the form because the action tells Apache to call file3.php when someone pressed the button to submit the form. This file introduces several concepts. First off, please note the use of two different HTML submit buttons. The web browser will send the value of whichever is pressed and not send data for any not-pressed buttons of type submit. That is the trigger for all of web programs no matter what language, what web server, or what architecture.

The new PHP-isms here are the declaration of an array and the use of the foreach loop. Programmers accustomed to C/C++ and such will be mystified by the array construct in PHP. It is an associative array, or text map. We use the numbers 0, 2, 4, 7, and 9 as indexes in our array; yet we also use "thanks" as an index. Indexes can be a number or a string. The => semantic lexeme as in 7 => " very " assigns the string " very" to the array to store at the index identified by the value 7. `foreach` is a handy iterator to allow each item in the $story array to be successively put into $words for handling.

For JSP or ASP Programmers

Synchronicity reigns. Just as C# mimicked Java, PHP has come to mimic JSP. JSP itself largely mimicked ASP until more advanced features such as templates were added to JSP. The divergences of PHP from JSP and ASP are that in PHP classes are first class citizens and, unlike JSP, PHP lacks strong data typing. In PHP one can refer to a class as part of a script and this is common practice. In JSP this practice (POJO's) was largely discouraged until the last few years. ASP was left behind in the Microsoft space just as many of their other technology religions have been: MFC, OLE, and COM. In the Java space JSP became out of vogue and large, ungainly frameworks like J2EE and Spring became popular. PHP doesn't play the games of technology led by the marketing department or technology by the trend. It simply provides a solid programming language and works. The goal of PHP developers is to get things done.

PHP Junior High School

Testing this out one will see the adjective gets printed two extra times at the end before and after the last entry in the $story array: `$story["thanks"]`. This needs to be cleaned up a bit. Also, the same adjective is used over and over. Let's support multiple adjectives. The visitor submits a web page with one adjective. What if we could remember that word and then let them submit another word? Once they have submitted enough adjectives then we could print the story. But how do you remember the words? The PHP script is run each time the web browser submits the page. Four techniques are used:

1) Store data in cookies. The data is stores on the user's computer and sent in with each web page submission.

2) Store the data on the created web page in an <input> of type "hidden". Keep adding to it or adding "hidden" fields. These will not show on the web browser visually but will be there if someone Views->Source for the web page. These will be sent with each web form post.

3) Store the data in a database. Use the visitors IP address or a cookie to determine an identifier for what to look up in the database.

4) Store the data in the "session" meaning it is maintained by the web server. The web server actually does something like #3 above but may store the session in a database or in its program memory. Obviously, if the web server is turned off then "session" data is lost from memory and, thus, a database can be more reliable. Plus, storing sessions in a database allows a cluster of webservers, also known as a farm, to work together and share the load of web visitors.

Web Programmers typically use the session. In PHP session_start() tells Apache to store data for the PHP program. The $_SESSION[14] array is used to exchange the data with Apache. So, we'll stick our data into the $_SESSION. We'll create an array called $inputs and store that array in the session array as "adjective_inputs".

```
<html><head><title>PHP is fast and easy</title></head>
<body>
<form action="file4.php" method="post"><br><br>
Enter an adjective: <input type="text" name="msg" size="30"><br>
<input type="submit" name="subbutn" value="Add">
<input type="submit" name="subbutn" value="Restart">
</form>
<? session_start(); // could be already auto started based on PHP settings
   $inputs = $_SESSION["adjective_inputs"];
   // print_r( $inputs ); // debugging. array printing funciton in PHP
?>
<?
$input = $_POST['msg'];
$submit_button = $_POST['subbutn'];

if( $submit_button == "Restart" )
{
  $_SESSION["adjective_inputs"] = null;
}
else if( $submit_button == "Add" )
{
  // $count = count($inputs, COUNT_RECURSIVE ); // PHP 5.1: always returns
the initial array count. Use another technique.
  $count = $_SESSION["adjectives_count"];
  // echo "<br>-- $count adjectives in \$inputs -- <br>"; // debugging
  if( $inputs == null ) {
       $inputs = array( 0 => $input );
       $count = 0;
  } else {
       $inputs[$count] = $input;
  }
  $count += 1;
  $_SESSION["adjective_inputs"] = $inputs; // store the adjectives back
```

---

14 See other session_ functions at http://www.php.net/manual/en/function.session-register.php

```
into the session
  $_SESSION["adjectives_count"] = $count;
  if( $count < 4 ) {
?>
<p><h3><?echo $input?>.<br>Please enter another adjective. You have
entered <?echo $count?> and 4 are needed.</h3></p>
<?
  } else {

  $story = array(0 => "It was the ", 2 => " of times. It was the ", 4 => "
of times. ", 7 => " and very ", 9 => " it seemed to everyone." );
  $story["thanks"] = "<br>Thank you for your words! ";
?>
 <br><center>
<?
  $input_index=0;
  foreach( $story as $words ) {
     echo $words;
     if( $input_index < 4 ) {
        echo $inputs[$input_index];
        $input_index++; // increment by one
     }
  }
  echo "<br></center>";
  }
} ifend
?></body></html>
```

file4.php

PHP High School

The modern PHP era arrived with PHP 3 with support for classes. Classes supplant the idea of using files to organize functions into manageable groups. Classes group similar functionality together and help make large projects manageable. Let's move our code into two different files. The first file will be a called storyteller.php and define a class named StoryTeller. The second file will be named wui.php and be very similar to our last file, file4.php, except use the StoryTeller class.

```
<?
class StoryTeller
{
  private $story = array(0 => "It was the ", 2 => " of times. It was the ", 4
=> " of times. ", 7 => " and very ", 9 => " it seemed to everyone." );
```

```php
    private $inputs = array();
    private $count = 0;

  public function AddAdjective( $input )
  { $this->inputs[$this->count] = $input;
    $this->count++;
    // echo $input . " is at " . $this->count;
  }

  public function StartOver()
  { $this->count = 0;
    $this->inputs = array(); // a new, empty array
  }

  public function GetStory() {
     if( $this->count < 4 ) {
        return "Please enter another adjective. You have entered " . $this->count . " and 4 are needed.";
     }
     return $this->MakeStory();
  }

  private function MakeStory() {
      $result = "";
      $input_index=0;
      foreach( $this->story as $words ) {
        $result = $result . $words;
        if( $input_index < 4 ) {
          $result = $result . $this->inputs[$input_index];
          $input_index++; // increment by one
        }
      }
      $this->StartOver();
      return $result;
  }

}
?>
```

A class named StoryTeller defined in a file named storyteller.php

Much may be seen in an example class. The private keyword prevents any code outside of this class from accessing the private data or private functions of this class. For instance, the function MakeStory() cannot be accessed from elsewhere. The data variables at the top may be accessed from within a function in the class. Note how the $ character moves to before the `this` keyword. Variables must be preceded with the `this` keyword. The `->` is used to specify the data within this instance of a class. If more than one StoryTeller object was made then more than one set of the data would exist. Functions may return a variable or may not. AddAdjective() does not return anything. MakeStory() does. GetStory() calls the MakeStory() function.

In order to use this class we have created a separate graphical user interface file called wui.php for web user interface. The file wui.php will create the HTML and will use the class to process the adjectives and create the story.

```php
<html>
<head><title>PHP is fast and easy</title></head>
<body>
<form action="wui.php" method="post">
<br><br>
Enter an adjective: <input type="text" name="msg" size="30">
<br>
<input type="submit" name="subbutn" value="Add">
<input type="submit" name="subbutn" value="Restart">
</form>
<? require "/var/www/html/storyteller.php"; // define the StoryTeller class
   session_start(); // could be already auto started based on PHP settings
   $teller = $_SESSION["mystory"];
   if( $teller == null )
   { $teller = new StoryTeller;
     $_SESSION["mystory"] = $teller; // store the object & it's data
   }
?>
<?

$input = $_POST['msg'];
$submit_button = $_POST['subbutn'];

if( $submit_button == "Restart" )
{ $teller->StartOver();
}
elseif( $submit_button == "Add" )
{ $teller->AddAdjective( $input );
  echo "<br></center>";
  echo $teller->GetStory();
  echo "<br></center>";
}

?>
</body>
</html>
```

The file wui.php

This file is even more interesting. The code is much cleaner and more maintainable. The behavior of the story generator can be coded separately and independently of the behavior of the web page code. The trick used here is the only thing stored in session is an instance of the StoryTeller class. An instance is also called an object. The object has data space for the variables of the StoryTeller class: `$count`, `$story`, and `$inputs`. By saving this in the session we can keep the data around across web page requests. The line `$teller = new StoryTeller;` creates a new instance of the StoryTeller class. Functions in the object are called with the `->` operator such as in `$teller->StartOver();`.

PHP College

Ok, we're ready for college. We can now move around in PHP and have seen if statements, functions, variables, and classes. An exercise for the reader is to turn the application into a multi-user Mad Lib application. One approach is to simply make the data in the StoryTeller class static. Static means it only is stored once within the running program (Apache) no matter how many instances (objects) are created. That approach is very unpopular. The other approach is to store the data in a database. Refer to existing PHP code for examples for accessing a database. Much of the existent Joomla! code uses a helper class provided with Joomla! and called mosDBTable. Refer to it for database example code. It is located in:

    `includes/database.php`

Also see the specific implementation for MySQL in the file:

    `includes/database.mysqli.php`

Normally PHP has functions for accessing the MySQL relational database system compiled into it as part of its binary module used by Apache; thus, various functions to interact with MySQL are just added to the PHP file and called as if they were local functions within that file. The normal run of events is to connet to the database, submit some SQL and receive responses, and to disconnet from the database. For instance, see the documentation for the function to connect to the MySQL service at:

    `http://devzone.zend.com/manual/view/page/function.mysqli-connect.html`

In JSP and other WebApp servers a concept of data space shared across all PHP scripts on the server exists. No such $_APPLICATION or $_CONTEXT exists yet for PHP. Therefore a database, file-based, shared-memory based, or other such approach may be necessary. Much more can be said about PHP but the best way to learn it is to write some PHP code to work with Joomla!.

The Real World: Joomla!

A quick look around the Joomla! directory tree shows lots of opportunities to explore some great code. Consider its libraries subdirectory. For instance, the pear subdirectory contains the PEAR: PHP Extension and Application Repository. Within this one can see Joomla! pre-installs some classes such as those for handling Mime types. Mime types are an important part of labeling HTML content and other web content; Joomla! doesn't build its own, it builds on the work of others. Many components reuse the PEAR library as well. Several other libraries can also be seen. The phpgacl is covered somewhat in the Security discussion. patTemplate is covered somewhat in the Templates discussion.

In the libraries/joomla and the includes subdirectories of the main Joomla! directory are the bulk of the Joomla! implementation files. In Joomla! 1.0 a lot more is in the includes subdirectory whereas in Joomla! 1.5 a lot of the code is in the libraries/joomla subdirectory. For instance the file includes/database.php can be a great place to start to see how Joomla! interacts with its database. For instance, the database::database function in Joomla! 1.0 uses the compiled-in function mysql_connect() to connect to the database. This code has moved to libraries/joomla/database/database/mysql.php in Joomla 1.5. A quick way to start looking though the code is to search for where a function is defined. In Linux one could use the "grep" command while in Windows one could use the "find" command. Grep is quite a bit more powerful than "find"; so often people install "Unix tools" on Windows. Open a prompt and change to the Joomla directory. Then run:

```
grep mysql_connect -R *
```

Modules

Modules are the pieces which make up most of the web pages. For instance, the home page shows a Main Menu, a User Menu, Latest News, Polls, and News Flashes. These are all Joomla! Modules. By adding and enabling Modules one can determine what appears on every web page.

Add a Module

1. Bring up the Administrator area of Joomla!
2. Select the menu option Modules->Site Modules
    1. There one sees the many already configured modules.
3. Click the New button.
4. Enter a title such as ImageModule
5. The Position determines where it appears on each web page. Leave the selection as left.
6. Menu Item Links determines when it is displayed. Leave All selected.
7. In the big box at the bottom for "Custom Output" Content enter an image.
    1. Click the "Insert/edit image" button below the word Styles and just to the right of the anchor button.
    2. Enter a URL such as /bizapps/joomla/images/monstericon.png.
    3. Enter other information and click Insert.
    4. Back at the top on the right click the Save button.
8. Visit the home page and refresh if needed. The image will appear.
9. Select the ImageModule again and change its Position to right and its Menu Item Links to mainmenu1 -registration (or any other menu entry added so far).
10. Visit the home page and refresh if needed. The image will appear when you click the Registration link and be blank otherwise.

No PHP Allowed Here

One might attempt to run a PHP script as part of the Module. For instance, one might attempt to edit the HTML for the module using the "Edit HTML Source" button to the right of the question mark in the blue circle and then try to type in a PHP script like

    <% phpinfo(); %>

but what would happen? When the HTML is saved then Joomla! devours it. For security and maintainability PHP is not allowed to be added to Modules as part of the HTML. A hacker may even try to update the record stored in the Joomla! database only to find it does nothing when the home page is refreshed and is again devoured by the Module editor.

```
mysql
mysql> show databases;
mysql> use bizapps_joomla;
mysql> show tables;
mysql> select title from jos_modules;
mysql> select * from jos_modules
           where title like 'RunSomePHP%';  // or whatever the Module is named.
mysql> update jos_modules
           set content = 'Let&#39;s run some PHP: <? phpinfo(); ?>  OK, did it run?'
           where title='RunSomePHP';
mysql> quit
```

Refreshing the front page as well as reviewing the Module in the Administrator area reveal PHP insertion is artfully thwarted; so, to run a dynamic script on the server to produce the web page content then one needs to use a Component or to author a Module from scratch outside of the Administrator area.

Code a Module

The fastest way to add custom code to Joomla! is to write a module. Modules are simple. They represent content on a web page. A module gives you a way to run that bit of PHP to create the text or web page content you are adding to a web page. The module itself is a simple PHP code file. It is accompanied by an XML file specifying its name and other info for installation. The name of this example file is mod_sayhello.xml. The module and its installation file must start with mod_.

```xml
<?xml version="1.0" ?>
<mosinstall type="module">
    <name>SayHello</name>
    <creationDate>12/Dec/2006</creationDate>
    <author>Max Weber</author>
    <copyright>CopyLeft</copyright>
    <authorEmail>MaxWeber@UnitedSWE.com</authorEmail>
    <authorUrl>http://www.serviza.com/</authorUrl>
    <version>1.0</version>
    <description>Demos using PHP within the web page.</description>
     <files>
         <filename module="mod_sayhello">mod_sayhello.php</filename>
     </files>
</mosinstall>
```

An example installation file for a module.

The other file is the Module code itself. It is whatever PHP code you want to provide. This example simply prints out "Hello World" to the page. It also uses PHP to list out the file name of the code being run.

```php
<?php
/**
* @version 1.0 $
* @package SayHello
* @copyright CopyLeft
* @license http://www.gnu.org/copyleft/gpl.html GNU/GPL
*/
defined( '_VALID_MOS' ) or die( 'No browser access permitted.' );
?>
<h1>Hello World</h1>
<? echo 'hello from echo';?>
<? print "Hello from print<br>";
    print "This message is from the PHP file ". __FILE__;
?>
```

Example module PHP file, named mod_sayhello.php.

Zip It

Create the two files. Put them in a directory named like mod_sayhello. Then compress the directory into an archive in zip or other format. This archive is what is disseminated for installation. The installation is simple in Joomla!. Simply click on Installers->Modules, Browse for the file, and click the "Upload & Install" button. If an error occurs then recall the files must be compressed as part of a subdirectory named like mod_sayhello.

In Joomla! 1.5 one must enable backwards compatibility to be able to show this module. First select the menu option "Site->Control Panel" and then click on the "Global Configuration" button. Finally, click the tab labeled Server and click the Yes radio button beside "Enable Legacy Mode". Click Save. Now the module may be installed. Click Extensions->Install/Uninstall then Browse for the file and click "Upload File & Install". Joomla! 1.5 uses a compatibility mode to run older modules.

Publish It

The module is initially unpublished. One needs to publish it. In Joomla! 1.0 simply select "Modules->Site Modules", check the box beside the new module named SayHello, and click the publish button at the top right. Look at the order and position columns to see where the module will appear. The default is to the left of the screen and at the very bottom.

View It

Simply refresh the home page to see the new module. By default it will be at the very bottom and on the left. You may notice some funny business with the formatting as the filename may over-run into other parts of the page. This is the risk of using DIV tags from HTML as a way to lay out a web page. Both Joomla! 1.0 and Joomla! 1.5 will require you to take care in the formatting and manage this yourself in the HTML code you create.

Gotchas

Don't get got. Here's one possible issue: clicking to Delete the module really doesn't delete the module files or directory in both 1.0 and 1.5. Solution: Delete the folder manually. E.g.

```
rm -fr /var/www/html/bizapps/joomla15/modules/mod_sayhello/
```

Here's a niggling bug in 1.5. The Publish button is not enabled immediately after the module is installed. Even though one checks the box beside the new module one must use the "Publish" word link. After the page redisplays then the button becomes enabled. Go figure. Maybe this one will be fixed in the final 1.5 release.

Joomla! 1.5 Example

Let's turn Legacy Mode back off. Click No for "Enable Legacy Mode" on the Server tab of the Global Configuration. Save it. Refresh the home page. Notice the error message comes from our module. This is from the line:

```
defined( '_VALID_MOS' ) or die( 'No browser access permitted.' );
```

so right away we know VALID_MOS must not be part of the standard Joomla! 1.5 variables. It must only be defined when we are running Joomla! 1.5 in legacy mode. A quick look a Module installed with Joomla! 1.5 will help us revise our code. The file

```
/var/www/html/bizapps/joomla15/administrator/modules/mod_latest/mod_latest.php
```

has the lines:

```
14    // no direct access
15    defined( '_JEXEC' ) or die( 'Restricted access' );
```

so we can see the new variable is named _JEXEC rather than _VALID_MOS. One can see that _JEXEC is indeed defined in index.php in Joomla! 1.5. Let's change our code and try again. Simply edit our mod_sayhello.php file in-place in the directory:

```
gedit /var/www/html/bizapps/joomla15/modules/mod_sayhello/mod_sayhello.php
```

and replace the word _VALID_MOS with the word _JEXEC. Now refresh the website. Once again the module displays. So, legacy mode is simply a way to allow older variables to be used.

A simple code change can make our simple Hello World example work properly in both places. If _VALID_MOS is not defined then perhaps we are running in Joomla! 1.5 so check for _JEXEC. If neither is defined, then we have an unsupported access scenario. The new code becomes:

```
defined( '_VALID_MOS' ) or defined( '_JEXEC' ) or die( 'Restricted access' );
```

Legacy Mode

A quick look into includes/application.php shows how the Legacy Mode changes the code being run.

```
function setLegacy($force = false)
{
        $config = & JFactory::getConfig();
        if ($config->getValue('config.legacy') || $force) {
                jimport('joomla.common.legacy');
        }
}
```

Modules

The file libraries/joomla/common/legacy/classes.php is over 1850 lines of code to support older versions of Component, Modules, and Mambots/Plugins. For instance, the mosCommonHTML class has been superseded by a new JCommonHTML class in Joomla! 1.5. The loadOverLib function should now be used from JCommonHTML.

In general, most older Components and Modules will work in Legacy Mode. If one is releasing code for both Joomla! 1.0 and Joomla! 1.5 then one will have to run in Legacy Mode; or else create two separate code bases.

AdSense Module (ClickSafe - Special Edition)

http://www.joomlaspan.com/joomla-downloads/startdown/14/

Google AdSense allows you to sell part of your web page for advertising. Google crawls your web page and dynamically determines what ads to show. People pay Google around 40 cents to $1 or more per click in the AdWords program. A well-worded ad may convert 1 in 10,000 people to click on the link. That is, once you have 10's of thousands of hits to your site then you might reasonably expect to make some money from the advertisements. Old-school advertisers such as TV or print make you pay for impressions rather than performance. Of course, even once someone "clicks through" you still have no guarantee they will buy your product as they still may click away very fast as that is the nature of the web. The AdSense Module makes it easy to work with Google in this program.

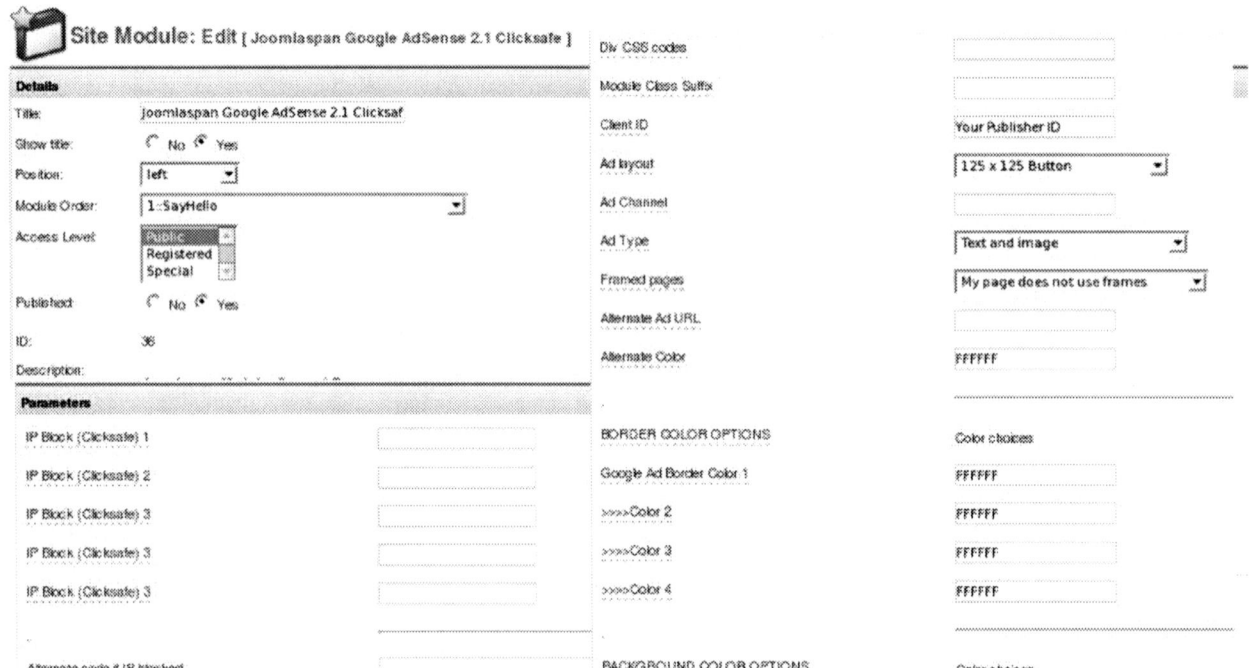

Screenshot of some of the AdSense Module configuration parameters.

The world of click-throughs harbors some dark lurkers as well. Imagine a hacker who writes a program to automatically click on a competitor's ads. The competitor is billed for clicks when, in actuality, these were programs and not people. This practice was the rage a few years ago and people setup websites hosting Google AdSense or other programs and then ran programs on other computers to click the ads so they would generate revenue. Today the accounting has become a little more advanced and repeated clicks from the same IP address are taken into consideration. The Clicksafe edition helps alleviate this risk by altogether blocking the Ads from certain IP addresses – your competitors for instance. You probably also want to block ads from your internal personnel as well since they are trying to be productive on the website and not browsing in search of other websites.

This module also has nice formatting features such as allowing the content to be aligned on the left, right, or center. It also can determine the size of the ads based on the format chosen. The module is for non-content areas such as menus; whereas another version is for content areas where articles could be found. This Module works with either 1.0 or 1.5 of Joomla!. To use this module in Joomla! 1.5 one must Enable Legacy Mode in the Global Configuration.

Google Adsense Revenue Sharing

http://www.justin-cook.com/wp/2006/04/03/free-joomla-module-adsense-revenue-sharing/

Justin Cook has actively updated the Google Adsense module to provide additional functionality and to enable revenue sharing. The main features added are:
1. Ability to specify a default AdSense ID
2. Ability to specify a default channel ID
3. Ability to specify ad impression sharing percentage (50%, 33%, 25%, 20%, 10%)
4. Ads may be blocked for up to 5 IP addresses – useful for the site administrator for instance.
5. Specify alternate code for blocked ads
6. Choose ad alignment
7. Choose ad type
8. Choose ad layout
9. Specify framed pages
10. Specify alternate ad URL
11. Specify alternate ad color
12. Specify up to 4 border colors, background colors, link colors, text, and URL colors.

Components

Components are "The Big Deal" for Joomla!. Components are where Open Source simply runs ahead of old school proprietary software. Sure, old school software allows extension with components but the level of power and ability to integrate absolutely by looking at the Open Source code just does not exist. For instance, when one wanted to add into an old school software package such as Microsoft's Systems Management Server then one had to go a-searching for documentation and was limited to the provided API's (connecting functions) the product allowed; in contrast, with Open Source one can do anything. Open Source is a world with no walls. You can do anything you want with Joomla! Components.

One Component is thought of as "active" when it is being specified for display in a web browser. In contrast, Modules can be grouped together on a web page. Some Modules – such as the latest news module – are paired with Components. The Module can show at any time and the related Component shows when it is linked to and requested.

Adding a Component

Adding a Component into Joomla! takes three steps. First, install the code. Second configure the component. Third add the component to a menu for it to be shown.

1) Install the code. This one's not too bad. Grab the components' zip or gz file from the net. Go into the Administrator area to install it. Go to the menu Installers->Components. In Joomla! 1.5 the menu for installing components is called Extensions->Install/Uninstall. Browse the file and click to Upload and Install the file. In Joomla! 1.5 one can also install a component by entering a web address, or URL, to it.

2) Configuring the component varies based on how complex the component is. To get to it one uses the Component menu and selects the new component. If it's not there, then the install failed. Look at the Apache log for details. E.g. tail -200 /var/log/httpd/error_log

3) This one's not so intuitive. The trick is to select the menu and then add something to it. E.g. Go to the menu option Menu->mainmenu. Click the New button on the upper right. From here one has three ways to choose to add the component. The first is the normal and standard way for many components. All of these have the same effect for many components: that is, clicking on the new menu listing will vector the user to a web page with the component web page instantiated.

   1. Click the radio button beside Component in the group called Components. This choice adds the component itself to the main menu so it would appear on the front page.

2. Click the radio button beside "Link - Component Item" in the group called Components. This choice adds a link to the component to the main menu and the link would appear on the front page.
3. Click the radio button beside "Link - Component Item" in the group called Links. This choice does the same thing as the previous one #3.

Using a Component

The steps #2 and #3 list configuring and connecting a component to the web page. As an example, let's add the business's contacts. The steps are to setup the Contacts Component and then to add it to a Menu.

Contact Category

1. Use the menu "Components->Contacts->Contact Categories" and add a new contact category with the New button.
2. Enter a "Category Title" such as "Contact Us" and a "Category Name such as "bizcontacts".
3. Select an image if you desire one.
4. Enter a message the user will see in their web browser such as "Please contact us for more information. Please choose from one of the contact options below."
5. Click the Save button. Remember it is on the upper right rather than at the bottom.

Contact Entries

1. Select the menu option "Components->Contacts->Manage Contacts".
2. Click the New button and add a contact. Save the contact.
3. Add another contact.
4. As you can see the new contacts are added and may be deleted by clicking the checkbox beside the contact's name and then clicking the Delete button.

Add to a Menu

Now that we have the contact category, let's add it to a menu on the website.

1. Choose a menu such as with the menu option Menu->topmenu. Here one can add entries to a menu. "topmenu" was chosen so the Contacts link will be at the top of the web pages.

2. Click the New button. Click the radio button beside **Component** and click Next.
   1. In the name field enter "Contact Us".
   2. For the Component listing choose Contacts.
   3. Click the Save button.
3. Refresh the home page and see the new menu option at the top.
4. Select it and then select the contact category to see the listed contacts.

Quite quickly and easily a new functionality is added to the website. Rather than managing contacts as a text HTML page one can use the included component to manage them more cleanly. Contacts may be added, changed, and deleted without ever having to write HTML code. Plus, the contacts may be connected to the website menus with ease. A Component provides a standard way to add functions; yet still allow a custom back-end way of manipulating the contact list or other data used and shown by the Component.

Joomla! Forms

This chapter quickly covers web-based forms in Joomla!. Several forms components allow you to quickly create a form for the user to fill in and to save their submission into a database for viewing later. perForms will create a table for you while MosForms works off of existing database tables.

perForms

perForms is an excellent Component for Joomla! for making forms for people to fill in on the website. It installs just as any other Component. Simply download it[15] from http://extensions.joomla.org. PerForms is authored by Ilhami Kilic and also administered by Jonah Braun.

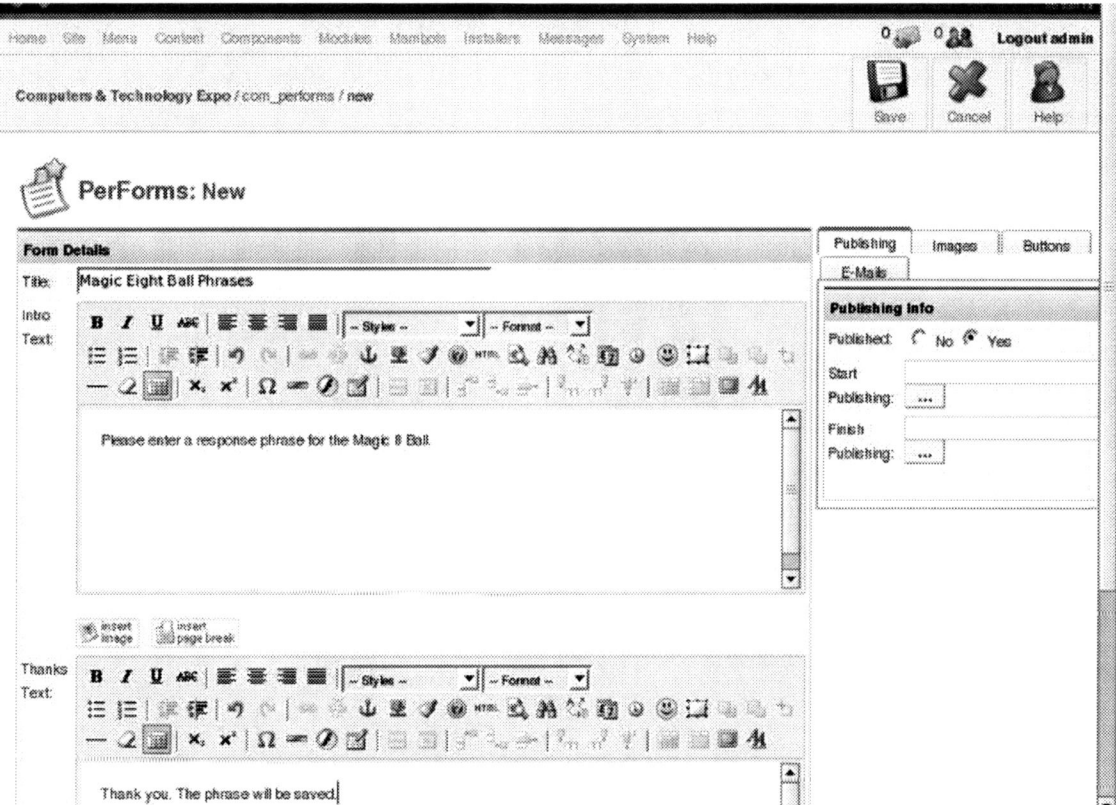

Screenshot of creating a new form in perForms.

The process to use it is straightforward. First one creates the form and enters the intro text and "thank you" text. To do this then click on Components->perForms and click the New button. Secondly one

---

15 Website security should always lock down the user permissions of webservers such as locking down Joomla to a user with limited rights. Refer to this perForms 1.0 security note: **http://xforce.iss.net/xforce/xfdb/27724**

enter the names and sizes of the fields to be typed into the form. Thirdly one gives a database name for the data to be stored upon entry. Finally one adds the component to the website. Later one can return to the Administrator area for Components and run a report of what data has been entered into the form.

Next, define the fields for the form. Click the "Edit Items" link in the listing.

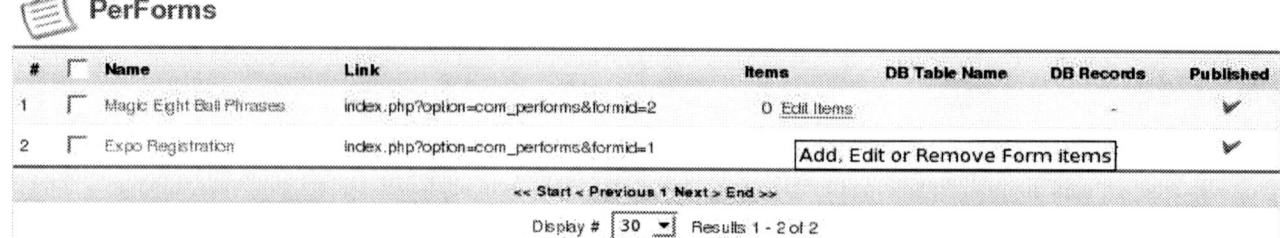

Screenshot of making a form with perForms.

Enter the items to be shown in the form. The data the user enters will be stored in a database. Later the admin can run a report and see what data has been entered. Click the "New Item" button to add an item. Notice in this case we made the form field "required" because we always want the user to enter something here.

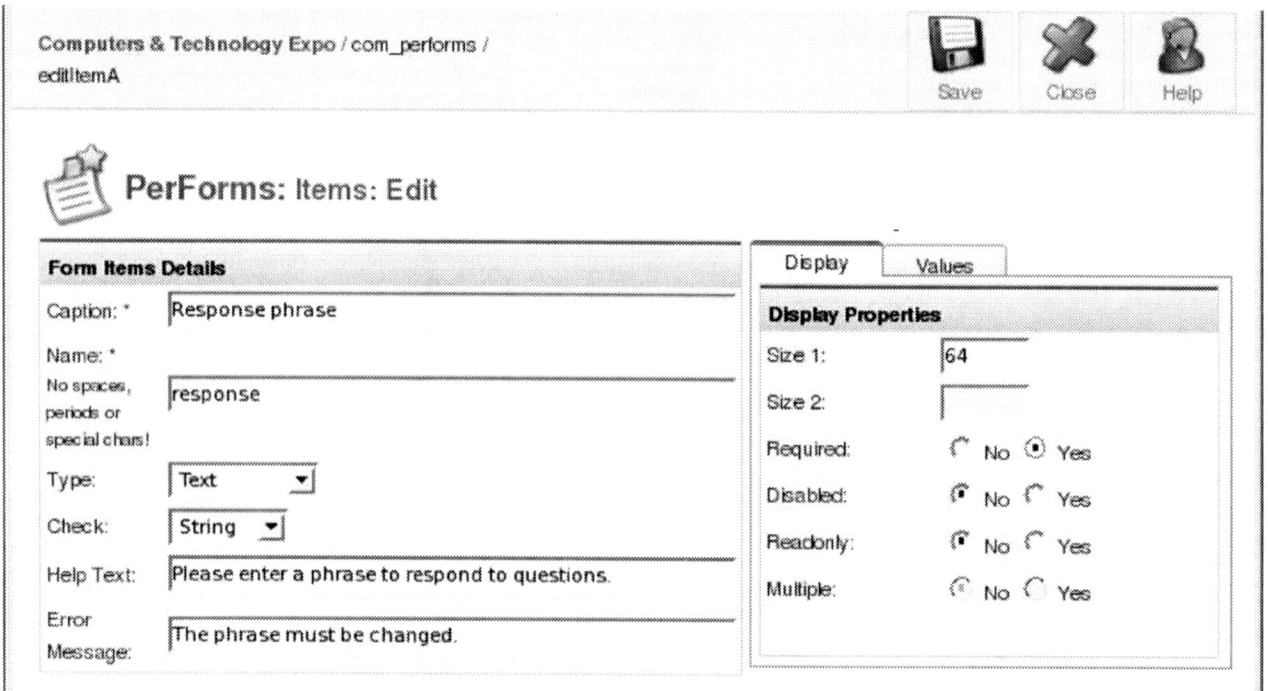

Screenshot of adding a form field in perForms.

Next we click the Close button on the Form field screen and return to the listing of forms. Once we are sure we've added all of the form fields we need then we click the Database button to create a

Joomla! Forms

database table for storing the entries. Check the box beside the new form and click the Database button. Enter a table name and click the Save button. The form is now created and should have a green checkmark nuder the column entitled Publish.

The final step is to add it to the website somewhere. These steps are the same as the "Adding a Component" steps in the Components chapter. Note, however, for perForms 1.* one has to tweak the actual source code. By the time you read this perForms 2 will probably be out of Beta and released but for completeness here are the steps. One edits the main PHP script file which will be called by Joomla!. This file is:

`/var/www/html/bizapps/joomla/components/com_performs/performs.php`

1) Hard-code formid in performs.php:
   ```
   24 if(empty($formId))
   25 $formId=1;
   ```
2) Fixed the SQL to have formId witha capital I rather than formid as documented elsewhere. Line 29, `WHERE id='$formId'`

Now perForms may be used. One fills in the forms and saves the data. Later the admin can run a report by clicking on the number of database records shown in the "DB Records" column for the form in the perForms Component Administration screen. A report screen such as below allows the data to be reported to the screen.

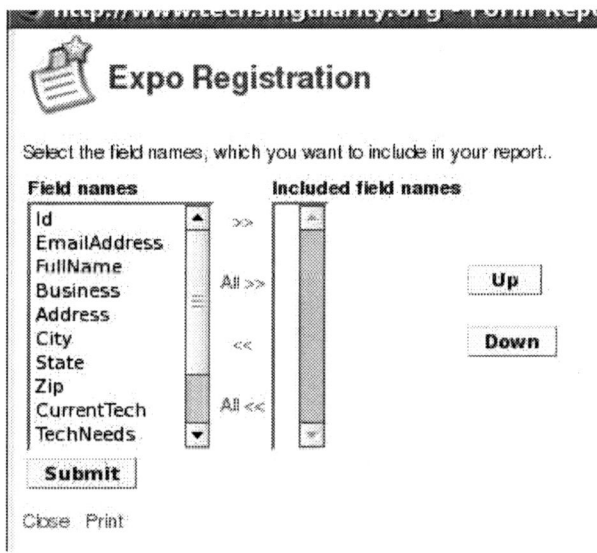

Screenshot of running a report in perForms.

Of course one can also look into the database and see the data added by perForms. The table will be the one named by you when you created the form.

83

Mosforms

http://mosforms.pollen-8.co.uk/ will offer it commercially in 2007 as "Fabrik".

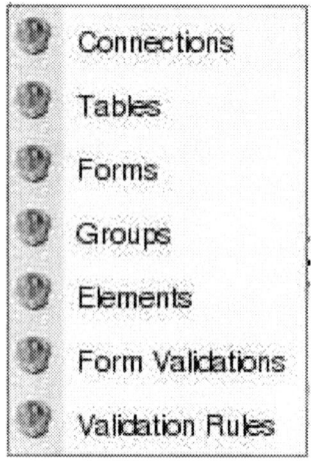

Mosforms is a swiss army knife for form entry as well as data analysis. Basically one selects a database and specifies a database table. Mosforms creates a web page form for a visitor to enter information. The visitor fills in the form and submits it to enter a new row to add to the table. In addition to creating the form, all of the data from the table can be listed on the screen.

One sees from the Component menu for Mosforms on the left how complete Mosforms truly is. The queries are nontrivial. The forms are complete and even include form validation. And the permissions and security for accessing the queries are sensible and secure.

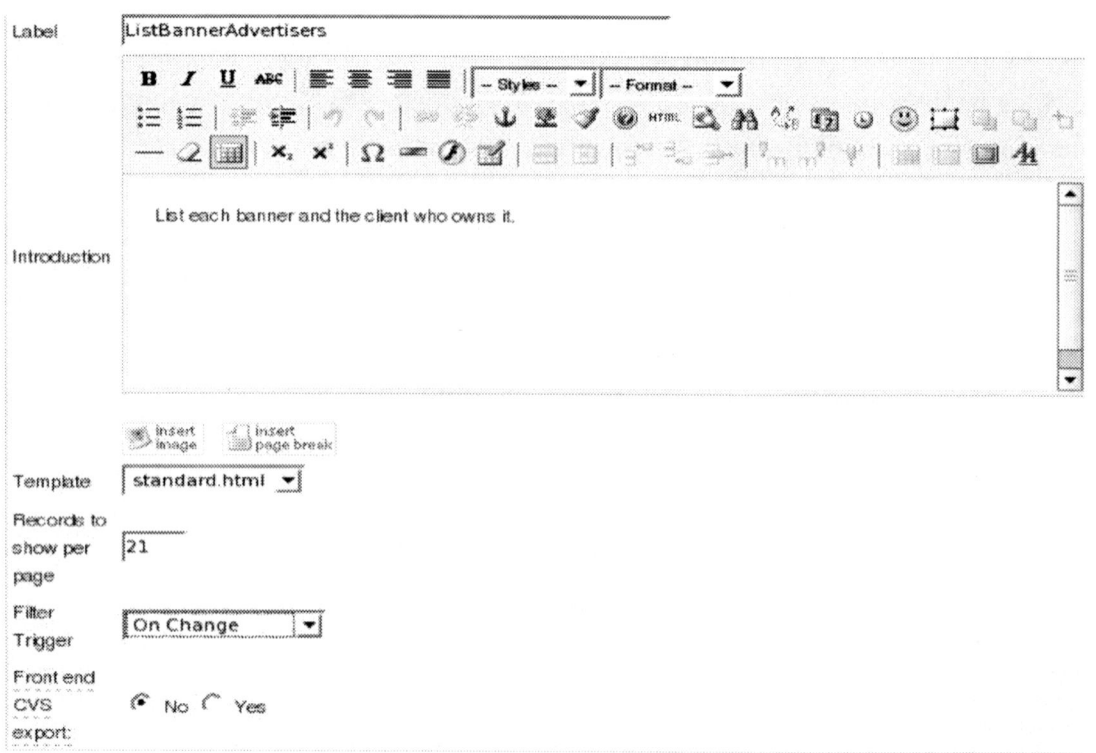

Screenshot of a new form in Mosforms.

Mosforms is not even limited to individual table as Mosforms knows how to write forms into multiple tables. While Mosforms does not allow a custom query to be entered, it does allow tables to be joined and filtered using a graphical user interface.

Joomla! Forms

Screenshot of a query joining two tables in Mosforms.

The "Link to menu" tab is a shortcut to allow the form to be accessed from a menu without the normal steps of configuring a new Component for a menu. The permissions to see the results of the data queries and to be able to add a new row are configured along with the table. CRUD - Create, Read, Update, and Delete – can each have a permission setting. Also, the permission can be based on a userid selected by the query and matching that of the registered user. This is the same as practices used in J2EE Portal applications. Wow, invest $100's thousands in a J2EE Web Application solution or run Joomla!. Hmm, tough one.

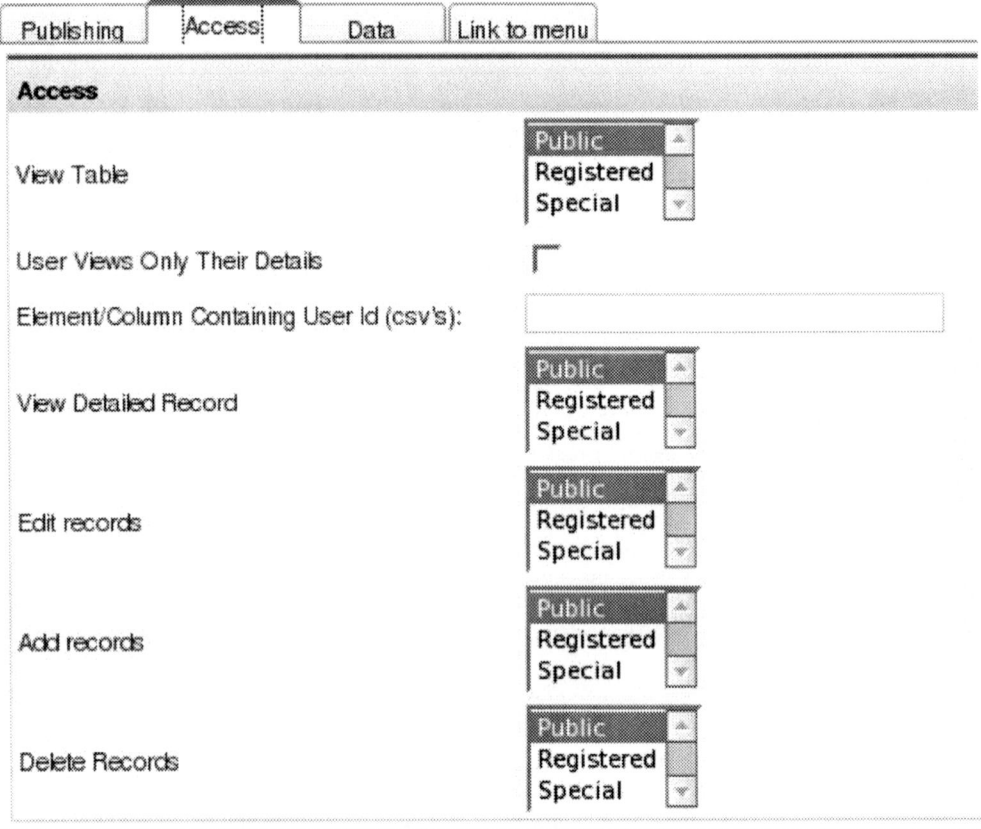

Screenshot of the permissions settings for the new form.

All bravado aside, Joomla! is feature competitive with enterprise appserver solutions. The availability of high quality, easy-to-use components makes Joomla! actually much faster for developing complex and feature-rich webapps. The practice of reusing components used on millions of other websites means higher quality and better feature sets may be leveraged.

Data Analysis

DBQ, Database Query

http://www.gmitc.biz

Fire up DBQ and put in a database query. Then the data can be shown on a web page. For example, the following query is first run in MySQL.

```
mysql
mysql> use bizapps_joomla;
mysql> select jos_bannerclient.name as Client, jos_banner.name as BannerName, imptotal, impmade, clicks, clickurl from jos_banner, jos_bannerclient where jos_banner.cid = jos_bannerclient.cid;
+-----------+------------+----------+---------+--------+----------------------+
| Client    | BannerName | imptotal | impmade | clicks | clickurl             |
+-----------+------------+----------+---------+--------+----------------------+
| DanaDevoe | danabanner |       0  |      5  |     1  | http://www.cnnfn.com/ |
| Goolge    | googlad    |       0  |      6  |     0  | http://www.google.com/ |
+-----------+------------+----------+---------+--------+----------------------+
2 rows in set (0.00 sec)
```

Next the query is copied for use in DBQ. Select "Components->DBQ Manager->Queries". Click the New button and add a new query. DBQ goes ahead and sets up the database information for the local Joomla database so we'll use it.

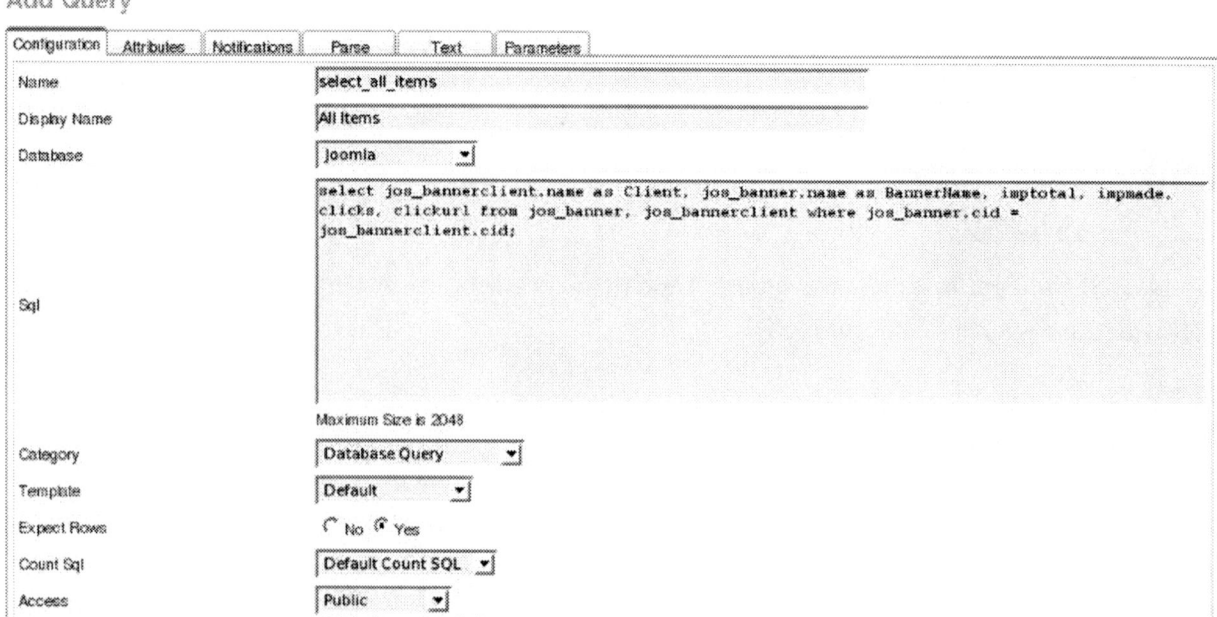

Screenshot of a new query in the DBQ Component.

Toby Patterson has also produced a very nice tutorial for DBQ which is available on his website. Simply put, be sure to publish the new query: click on the check-box beside it and click the Publish button. Then add the component to a menu. When the menu option is clicked the query will run and display the results:

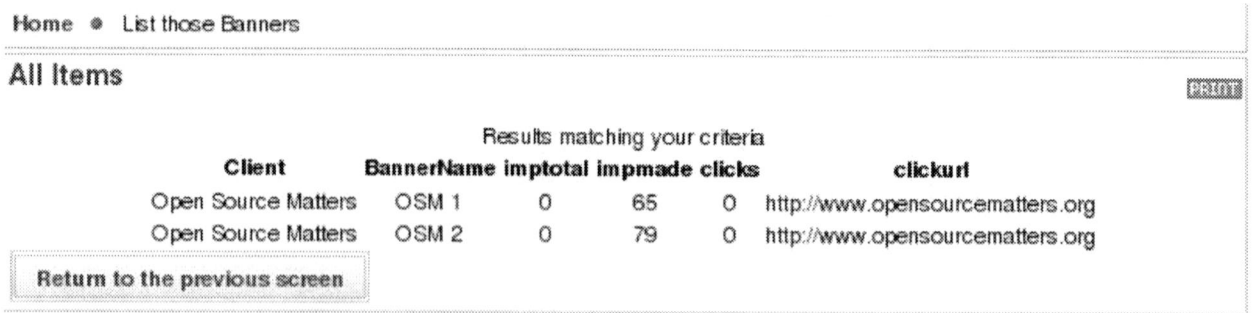

Screenshot of a database query and the results in Joomla! using DBQ.

DBQ has numerous other options such as the ability to define variables, substitions, regular expressions, statistics and much more. The output display of the queries can be configured to control what is displayed. Templates may be applied as well. Green Mountain Information Technology Consulting also provides consulting support and customization services for their module. The GPL version is backed by an even more extensive commercial version.

Data Analysis

DBQuery Configuration

#		ID	Name
1		56	Show Bottom
2		57	Default Language
3		58	Default Query Theme
4		59	Order Variables As Found in Query
5		60	Result Table is Sortable
6		34	Show Return Link
7		35	Show Form On No Results
8		45	Custom Code Enabled
9		46	Variable Template ID
10		50	Show Category Descriptions

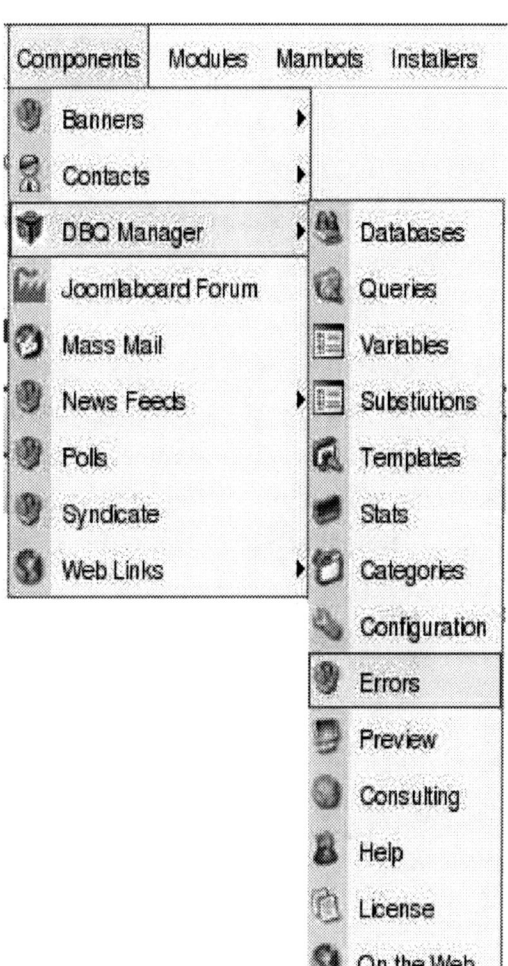

Website Statistics

1.0.3 and later versions of Joomla! have statistics built in with the standard install. These statistics are useful but limited. Enable Statistics gathering under the Global Configuration under the Statistics tab for Joomla! 1.0. For Joomla! 1.5 the Statistics are enabled on the Site tab of the Global Configuration. The statistics profiled are:

1. The search terms used. Go to Site->Statistics->Search Text to see these.
2. The type of Internet Browser that is used by visitors to the web site.
3. The type of Operating System (OS) that is used by visitors to the web site.
4. The top level domain - for example: .com, .org, .uk, .ru, - that is recorded from the IP Address of a visitor. Note this is the visitors IP Address not necessarily their country of origin.

Browser	%	#
Konqueror 3.0	0.40%	1
Konqueror 3.1	1.58%	4
Konqueror 3.3	0.79%	2
Konqueror 3.5	0.40%	1
Mozilla 2.0	0.40%	1
Mozilla 5.0	52.96%	134
Mozilla Firefox 1.0.4	0.40%	1
Mozilla Firefox 1.5.0.7	0.40%	1
Mozilla Firefox 1.5.0.8	1.19%	3
Mozilla Firefox 1.5.0.9	0.40%	1
Mozilla Firefox 2.0	0.40%	1
MS Internet Explorer 5.12	0.79%	2
MS Internet Explorer 6.0	22.92%	58
MS Internet Explorer 7.0	3.56%	9
Netscape 7.2	0.40%	1
Netscape 8.1.2	0.40%	1
Unknown	12.65%	32

Screenshot of some statistics gathered by Joomla!.

Additional tools for Apache allow much more detailed website trending. For instance, AWStats can produce nice charts of hits and other statistics.

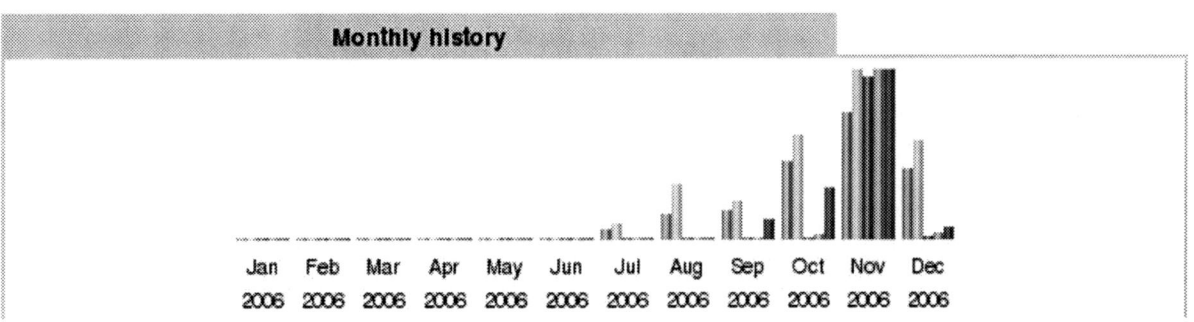

Screenshot of an AWStats report for Apache (not part of Joomla!).

BSQ Sitestats

http://developer.joomla.org/sf/projects/bsq_sitestats

BSQ Sitestats is under continued development and provides a complete analysis solution for website visits and visitors. Be sure to get the BSQ Sitestats Component and not the older Module. BSQ Sitestats requires the joomlaLib Component. joomlaLib is a set of classes with functions to make programming to Joomla! easier and more productive. It includes support code for AJAX, a progress bar, caching, Ip2City/ip2country, date/time conversions, Event logging, configuration manager, remote file opening (fopen+ curl), flash graphs, and safe file writing. joomlaLib is available from:

http://forge.joomla.org/sf/go/proj1846

To say BSQ Sitestats is a complete solution is an understatement. Not much, if anything, has been left uncovered. The only other setup step is to manually edit the index.php file of Joomla! to add the hit tracker for BSQ Sitestats. The code to add it provided as part of the installation of the BSQ Sitestats component and must be copied and added to index.php. Adding it at the very end of the file works fine.

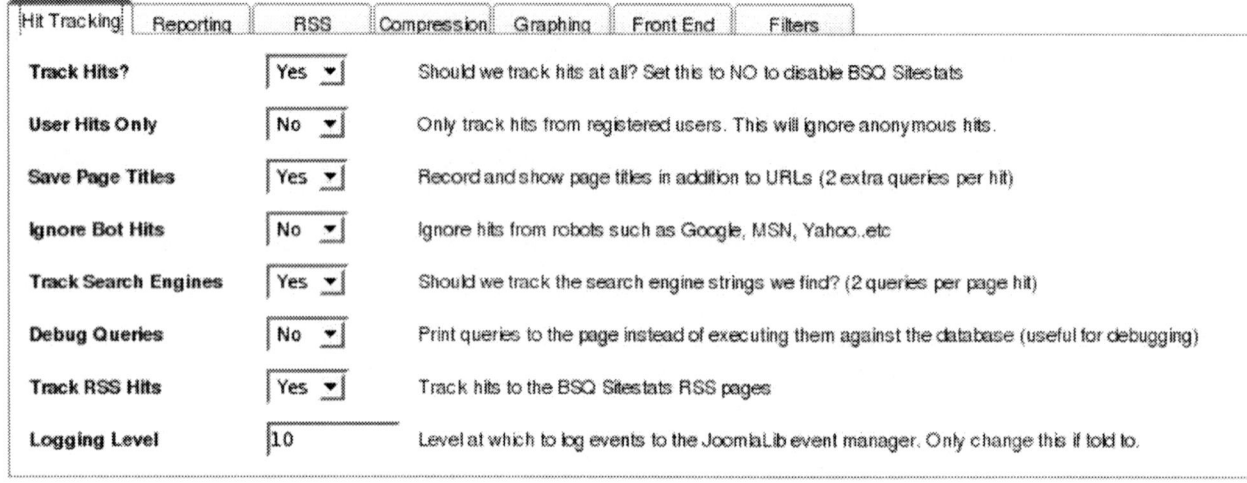

Screenshot of some configuration options in BSQ Sitestats.

Screenshot of the basic report in BSQ Sitestats.

Document Management

http://forge.joomla.org/sf/projects/docman

DOCMan

DOCMan adds document management to Joomla!. Specifically, files may be uploaded and access to them may be controlled.

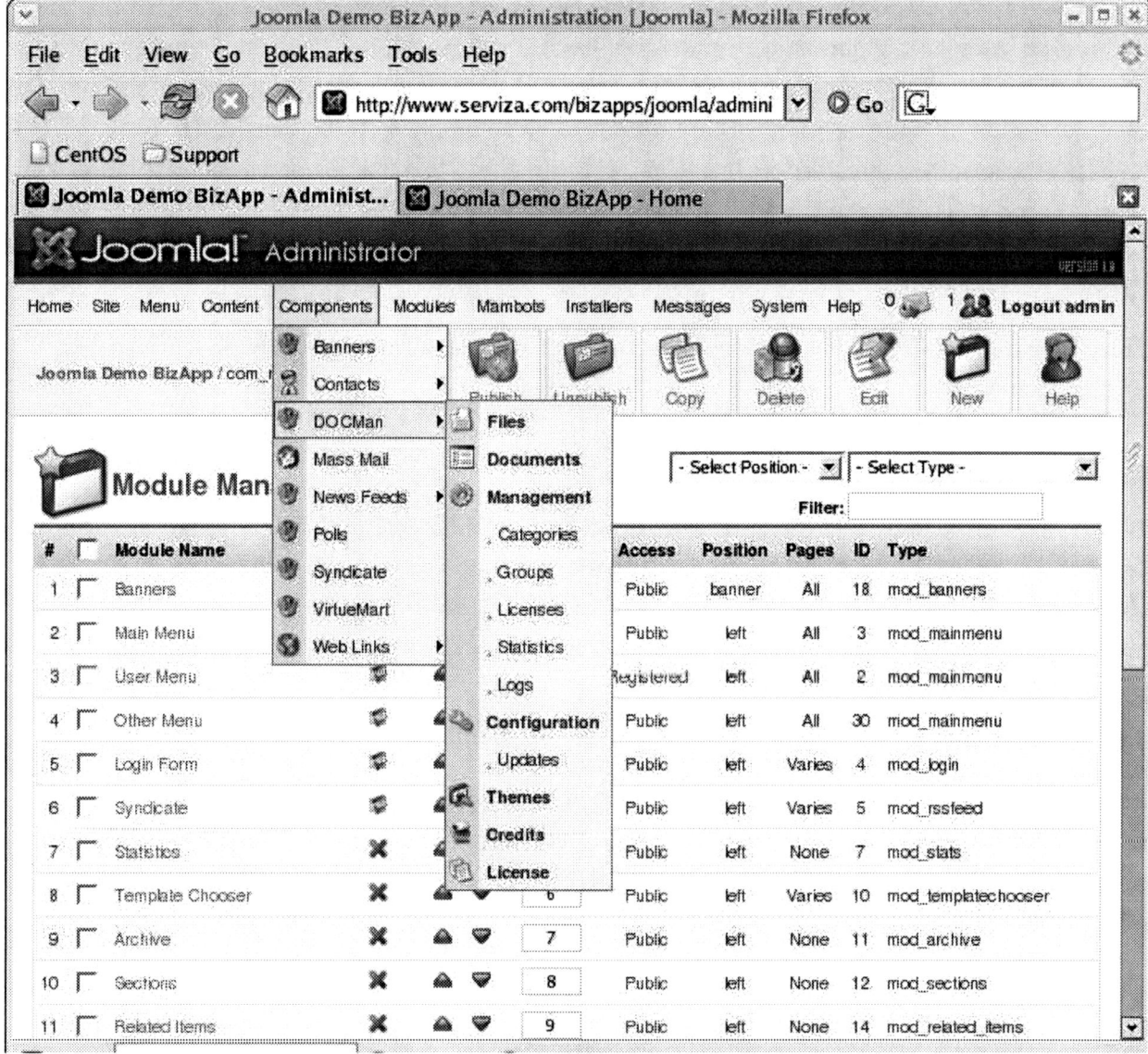

Screenshot of DOCMan within Joomla!

Install the component in the normal way. Then the first task is to observe the directory where files may be stored and other settings for managing the files. Use the menu option Components->DOCMan->Configuration. You will notice a directory for the files to be uploaded to on the server. For instance:
`/var/www/html/bizapps/joomla/dmdocuments`

Click on the tab labeled Upload. Notice the "Extensions allowed" is set to zip|rar|pdf|txt. You may want to allow XML files or ODT files to be uploaded so change this to zip|rar|pdf|txt|xml|odt. Click the Save button. Notice many other settings for controlling what files may be uploaded. The big idea is one would not want PHP or other dynamic files to be allowed because a hacker may upload such a file and then use the web browser to enter the web address of the file and launch it. The default configuration for DOCMan does not allow PHP files to be uploaded; however, in the Administrator area an administrative user can upload such files. Other users will not be able to do so on the website. One idea to further ensure safety is to specify a directory such as /var/dmdocuments when that is not a directory under Apache so Apache will never execute files in that directory.

Categories

Use the Components->DOCMan->Management tab and click on the categories button. Add a new category for documents.

Files

Users may be allowed to upload files from the front end website based on the Configuration settings for DOCMan. To upload a file in the Administrator area one simply clicks on Components->DOCMan->Files and then clicks the Upload button. Right away one will see a link to "Make a new document entry using this file.".

Files to Documents

Users see Documents on the web site. Authors upload Files in the Administrative area or on the website. A Document should be created for each File to be seen on the website. This layer of indirection allows documents to move through a publication workflow and allows permissions to see, edit, and delete the Document to be maintained separately from the File.

Workflow

DOCMan implements a traditional document workflow. Documents may be approved. Documents may be published or unpublished.

Gotcha

In PHP 5.1 for instance DOCMan has a bug to be fixed. First one will add it as a Component to a menu and try to click that menu option on the home page. The browser will display a blank, empty page. What's wrong? Where do you look? In the Apache log file of course. On FC6 Linux one finds this file at /var/log/httpd/error_log for instance. A line like this will appear:

[Mon Dec 18 16:38:52 2006] [error] [client 127.0.0.1] PHP Fatal error: Cannot redeclare themeConfig::$details_homepage in /var/www/html/bizapps/joomla/components/com_docman/themes/default/themeConfig.php on line 36, referer: http://localhost/bizapps/joomla/index.php

The fix is to edit the file and comment out the offending code.

vi /var/www/html/bizapps/joomla/components/com_docman/themes/default/themeConfig.php

Comment out line 36 as follows:

```
//var $details_homepage = "1";
```

MjazTools Autopopulate For Docman

http://forge.joomla.org/sf/projects/mjaztools

MjazTools Autopopulate for DOCMan will import thousands of documents into Joomla! and DOCMan within a hour or so. This is an easy way to move an entire document repository to Joomla!. The settings which may be specified for Documents in DOCMan may be specified for the files to be imported. Also, certain file extensions may be skipped.

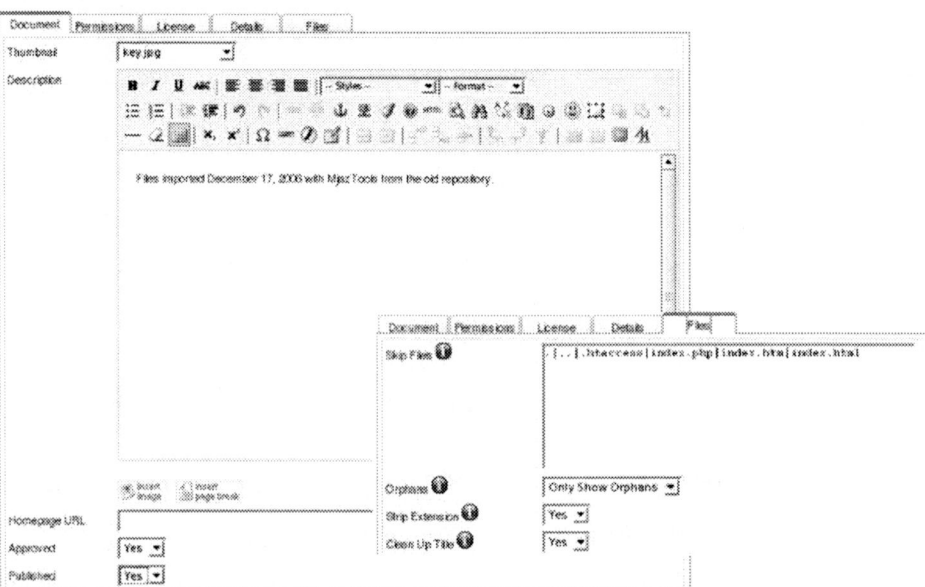

Screenshot of MjazTools to import files into a DOCMan repository.

Shopping Cart

VirtueMart

http://virtuemart.net/

VirtueMart (formerly mambo-phpShop) gives online storefront capabilities to Joomla!. Many reasons persuade one to run their own ecommerce storefront but the main reasons are ease of use and unlimited flexibility. While many Internet users are building their ecommerce solutions on osCommerce, VirtueMart allows one to run the complete website from within Joomla!. One benefit of osCommerce is, like Joomla!, osCommerce has tons of extensions so supports calculating shipping costs from UPS, USPS, and such as well as other features. Many of these features also exist in VirtueMart as porting between osCommerce and VirtueMart is easy because both are written in PHP.

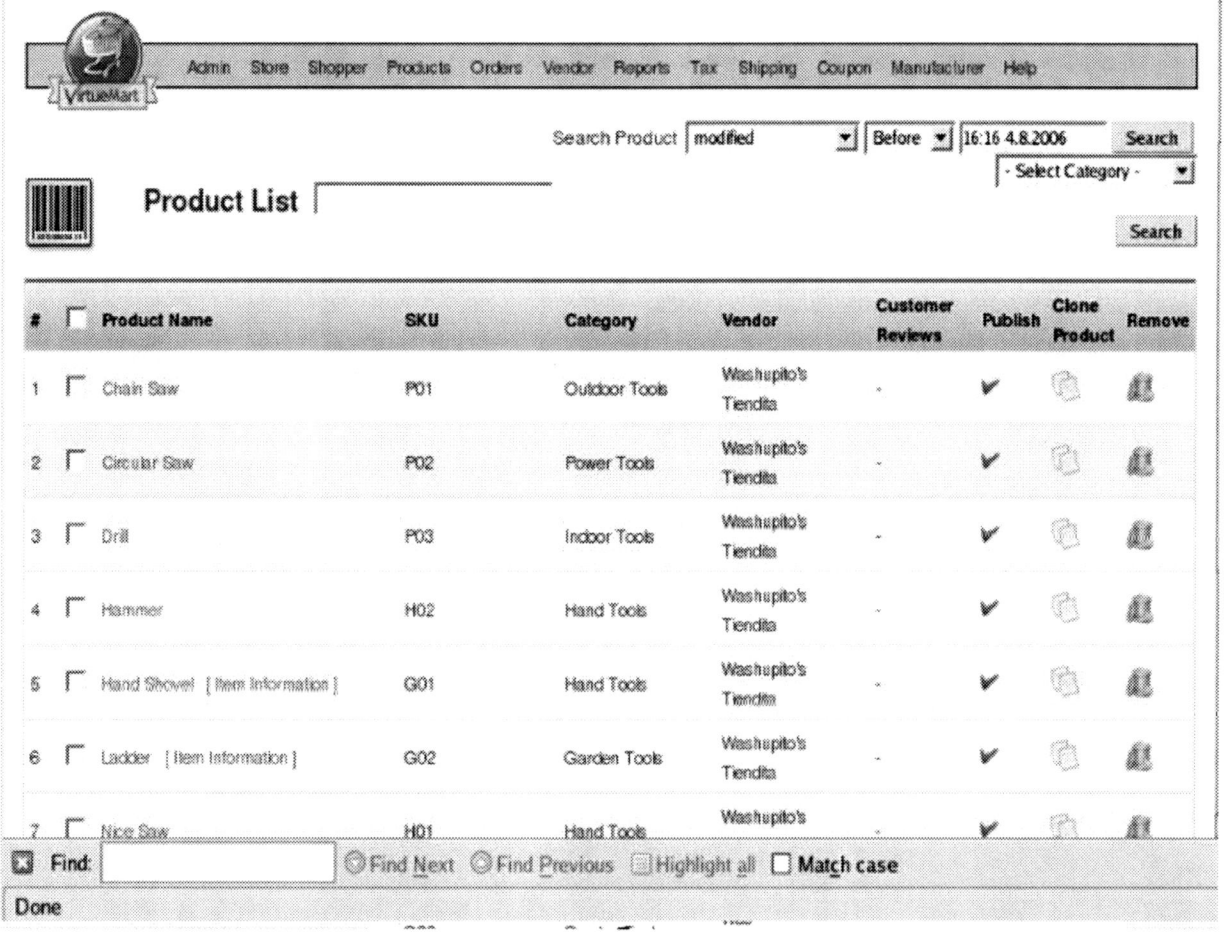

Screenshot of a list of products in VirtueMart within Joomla!.

Features of VirtueMart:

- VirtueMart can be used simply as a catalog without the features to buy online.
- Supports an unlimited number of products. Yahoo Stores[16] recently raised theirs to 50,000.
- Unlimited number of product categories.
- Ability to sell soft goods such as downloadable music, images, or software.
- Support for images and thumbnail images.
- Add Attributes like Size or Color to products.
- Product Discounts (percentage/total, time limited or not)
- Bulk upload and export to upload a product inventory from another database or file.
- Manage the Stock Level for Products and Items
- Automatically Notify Shoppers when a Product is back in Stock
- Running product "specials" to feature certain products.
- Shop statistics summary such as the number of customers and the number of orders.
- Integrated shipping calculations for USPS, UPS, Canada Post, and an extensible shipping API.
- Calculates sales tax based on shopper and store locales.
- Online credit card processing and other payment methods through several different vendors.
- Extensive searching capablities

Numerous add-ins for VirtueMart provide alot more functionality:

- <u>AJAX LiveSearch module for VirtueMart</u> displays items for sale as the user types. AJAX is an acronym for technology to retrieve data from the webserver without refreshing the whole web page. The list of items matching what is being typed is retrieved for a more powerful search.
- <u>Virtuemart Product Count Display</u> simply displays the number of products in your store.
- <u>Virtuemart Integrator</u> installs new features to make VirtueMart more search engine friendly to ensure your products can be searched and you can better control what the search engines index.
- Many other commercial modules exist to add functionality to VirtueMart.

SimpleCaddy for Joomla

http://boswachter.free.fr/

SimpleCaddy is a much simpler shopping cart for those selling only a few items.

---

16 See the cost analysis at http://www.marketingexperiments.com/online-marketplace/yahoo-stores.html

Administration

Joomap

http://developer.joomla.org/sf/projects/joomap

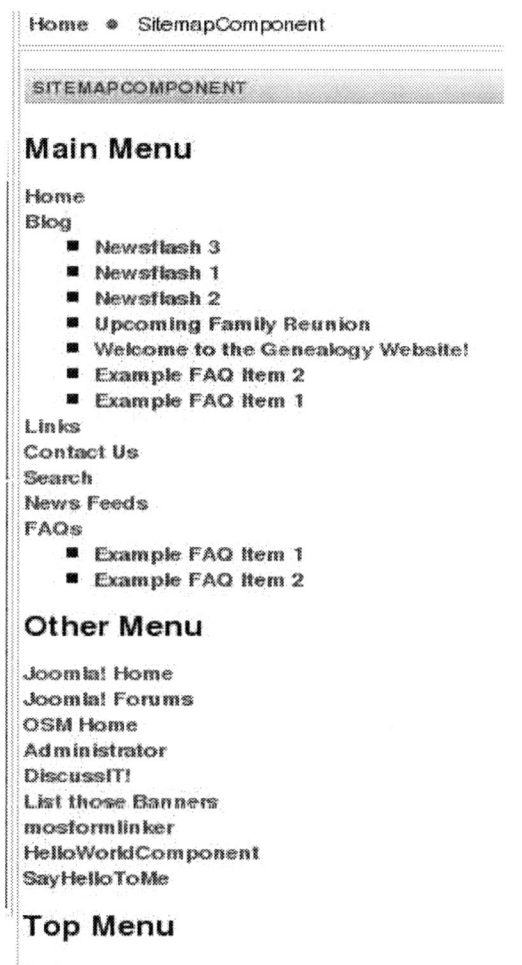

Joomap provides another way at looking at the sites content. All of the site is arranged into a hierarchical structure for immediately viewing everything. Joomap also can produce sitemaps in XML format which are useful for the search engines for setting how often various web pages are re-indexed; and, thus, limiting search engine traffic to occur only when needed. It can be used to generate a nice HTML listing of the web pages in a hierarchy, or tree, by adding this component to a menu for instance. It can also be used to generate the XML file required by search engines as a sitemap by using a URL such as:

http://localhost/bizapps/joomla/index.php?option=com_joomap&view=google

Note these do not have the update frequency elements so those can be added manually.

Community Builder

http://www.joomlapolis.com/

Community Builder extends the Joomla! user profile and security system. Key features include extra fields in profile, enhanced registration workflows, user lists, and connection paths between users.

Community Builder works with Joomla! 1.0 or 1.5.

Versioning

http://www.joomprod.com/

The Versioning Component adds simple Version Content Management to Joomla!. When a content is updated in the frontend, a backup version is saved. You can restore this version with the component and can even perform a replace all. Now users can edit content created by other users with the ability to roll-back if needed.

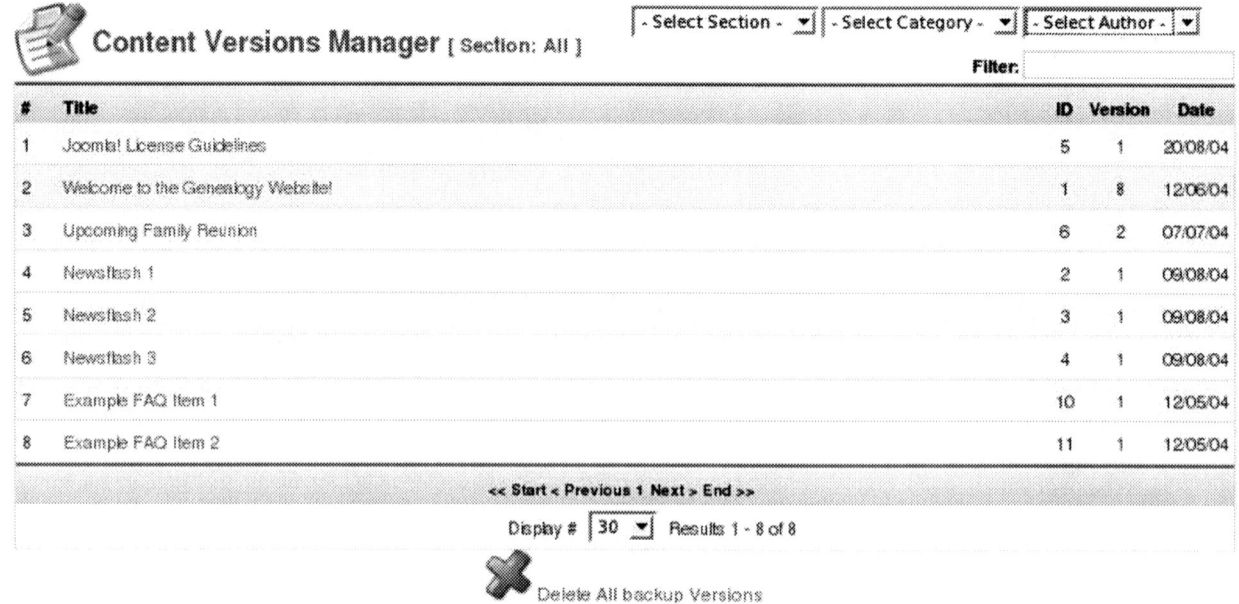

Screenshot of the Versioning Component in Joomla!.

LDAP Integration

LDAP Tools

http://developer.joomla.org/sf/projects/ldap_tools

LDAP Tools contains LDAP User Synchronization, LDAP User Authentication, and LDAP Single Sign On. It has been tested in a Novell eDirectory environment. Both Joomla 1.0 and 1.5 are supported.

Holodeck: LDAP Phonebook

http://mamboxchange.com/projects/holodeck/

Holodeck is a component to present a phonebook from an LDAP directory like Lotus Domino.

Photo Gallery

Numerous photo gallery extensions exist for Joomla!

- Gallery 2 Bridge works with the Gallery 2 software to integrate photos into Joomla!
- Exposé Flash Gallery allows you to create Flash-based slideshows from photos.
- RSgallery2's access control is presently independent of Joomla's. It also needs RSG2 1.10.4 to be installed for it to work. It installs as a module. Photos are shown using JavaScript.
- CBGallery Plugin adds photo gallery capabilities to Community Builder.
- Mehdi's Coppermine Bridge integrates Coppermine - the leading FOSS image gallery.
- zOOm Media Gallery uses a signed Java applet so it can read files from the local computer's disk. First click its Settings button and go to the Media tab and increase the "Medium - including images - max. size (in kB):" from 1024kB to smoothing larger if needed. Then simply add a Gallery and then add files to that Gallery with the zOOm Media Manager. A whole directory may be scanned or a file at a time may be added. ZOOm has numerous other features such as a "Lightbox" like a shopping cart where a visitor can mark photos and then download them all in a zip file.

Photo Gallery

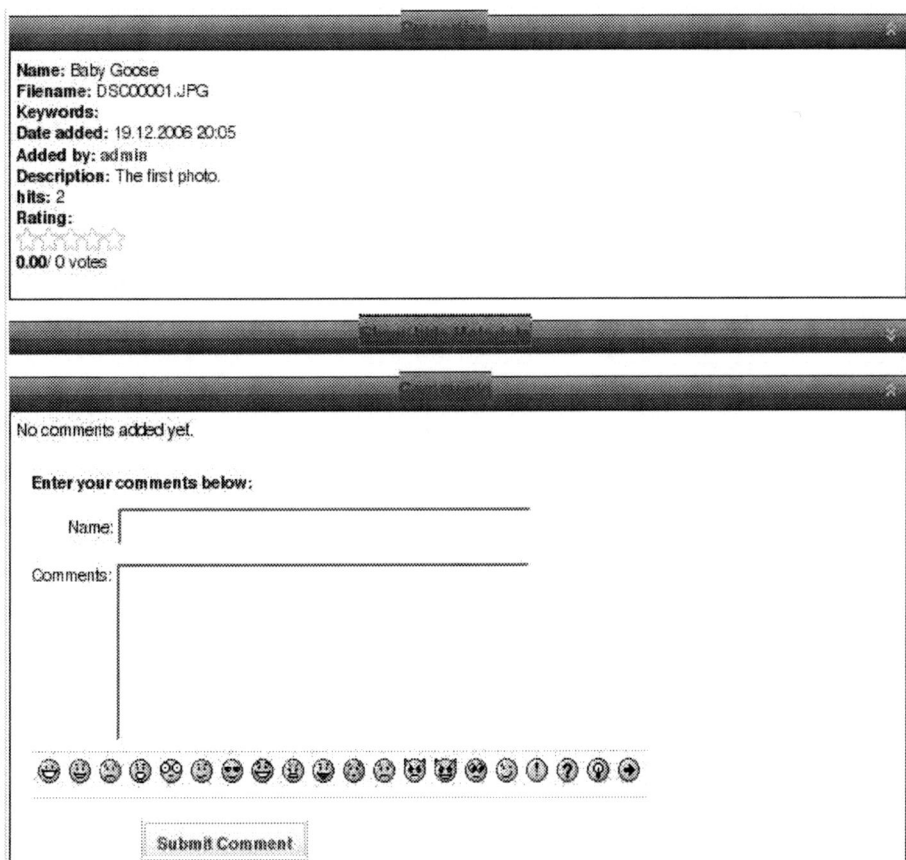

Screenshot of the comments screen for zOOm Media Gallery.

Search Engine Friendly Components

Joomla! Default SEF

The standard Joomla install already includes some niceness to ensure the search engines actually do their job and search your website. The issue is any web link with "?" in it is actually passing parameters. Two problem stop the engines from trying these links:

1) The range of acceptable parameters could be infinite. The search engine could get stuck reading randomly generated content or encircling itself by following every such link.

2) Some companies who have databases of data have set a legal precedent to disallow search engines from searching such data. Refer to the book, "The Invisible Web", for a survey of such sites.

Search engine optimizations are enabled with the SEO tab in the Global Configuration of Joomla! 1.x and in the Site tab of the Global Configuration of Joomla! 1.5.

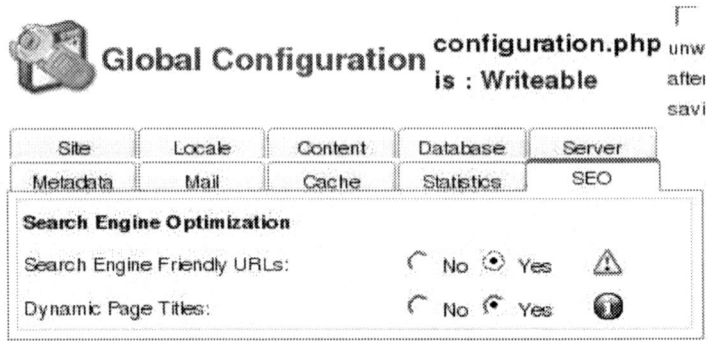

SEO configuration in Joomla! 1.x.

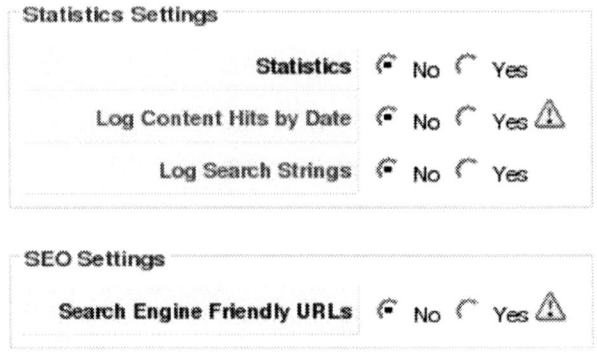

SEO configuration in Joomla! 1.5.

htaccess.txt

The following message appears when one first enables "Search Engine Friendly URLs" via the Global Configuration.

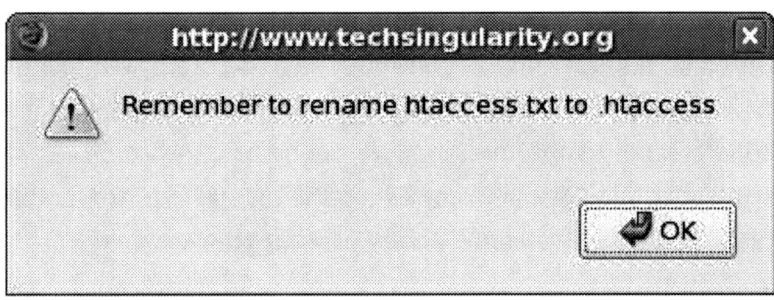

As it says, one should rename the .htaccess file. E.g.

```
mv /var/www/html/bizapps/joomla/htaccess.txt /var/www/html/bizapps/joomla/.htaccess
```

Look into this file and notice the bulk of it is settings for making the web addresses, or URL's, appear without ? and other parameter fields. The mod_rewrite Module of Apache is used to dynamically create URL's without ? and other HTTP query parameter characters.

Apache configuration has been discussed elsewhere but again comes into play when using the .htaccess file. One way of configuration Apache uses only configuration files such as httpd.conf and *.conf files in /etc/httpd/conf.d. Another option is to allow various directories to have their own configurations as specified by a .htaccess file in that directory. In our setup we are allowing .htaccess. We could also move the settings from this file and into a Directory in the Apache configurtation file, httpd.conf. To allow .htaccess files then one must change the default setting for the Apache Configuration file. The default is:

```
AllowOverride None
```

and we change it to allow .htaccess to do anything as follows:

```
AllowOverride All
```

We will also want to ensure the mod_write module is installed. Look for a line like the following in the Apache configuration file (In Windows the file will be named a DLL rather than a SO.):

```
LoadModule rewrite_module modules/mod_rewrite.so
```

OpenSEF

http://projects.j-prosolution.com/en/projects/os-projects/project-opensef.html

OpenSEF empowers your Joomla! website with simple web addresses, or URLs, so the search engines will fully index your website. It allows you to configure what the URL will be instead of a URL with a ? or a , or other query parameters which stop the search engines from visiting the page. It also supports converting he URLs to relative or to absolute; relative can be best for a website where more than one domain refers to the content; while absolute is often justified in order to steer others to provide an absolute link to your website content when they copy parts of your web page.

OpenSEF will replace a link like:

http://localhost/bizapps/joomla/index.php?option=com_content&task=section&id=1&Itemid=2

with a link like:

http://localhost/bizapps/joomla/content/section/1/2/

OpenSEF works with the default Joomla! SEF so the default SEF should be enabled. Also, the .htaccess file must be changed to work with OpenSEF. Comment out the lines in the section labeled "Begin - Joomla! core SEF Section" and uncommen the lines in the section labeled " Begin - 3rd Party SEF Section". The .htaccess file then becomes:

...

```
  #RewriteCond %{REQUEST_FILENAME} !-f
  #RewriteCond %{REQUEST_FILENAME} !-d
  #RewriteCond %{REQUEST_URI} ^(/component/option,com) [NC,OR]
  ##optional - see notes##
  #RewriteCond %{REQUEST_URI} (/|\.htm|\.php|\.html|/[^.]*)$  [NC]
  #RewriteRule ^(content/|component/) index.php
  #
  ########## End - Joomla! core SEF Section


  ########## Begin - 3rd Party SEF Section
  ############ Use this section if you are using a 3rd party (Non Joomla! core)
  SEF extension - e.g. OpenSEF, 404_SEF, 404SEFx, SEF Advance, etc
  #
  RewriteCond %{REQUEST_URI} ^(/component/option,com) [NC,OR]
  ##optional - see notes##
  RewriteCond %{REQUEST_URI} (/|\.htm|\.php|\.html|/[^.]*)$  [NC]
  RewriteCond %{REQUEST_FILENAME} !-f
  RewriteCond %{REQUEST_FILENAME} !-d
  RewriteRule (.*) index.php
  #
  ########## End - 3rd Party SEF Section
```

Search Engine Friendly Components

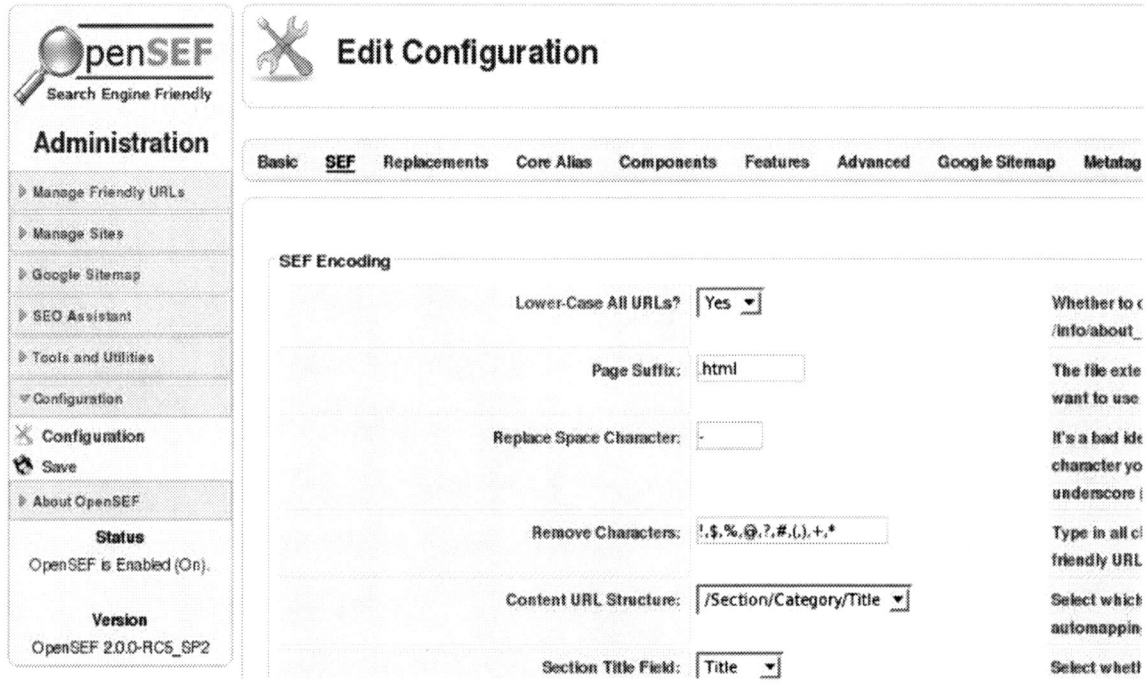

Screenshot of SEF configuration in OpenSEF.

That is about it. Some gotchas are that mod_rewrite must be installed in Apache and that htaccess files must be enabled. refer to the .htaccess section above for more information.

OpenSEF has so many features and useful tools you can spend several days simply exploring it all. consider the tools in the SEO Assistant. These allow search information about a site to be retrieved, keywords to be managed, and other Search Engine Optimization work to be quickly performed.

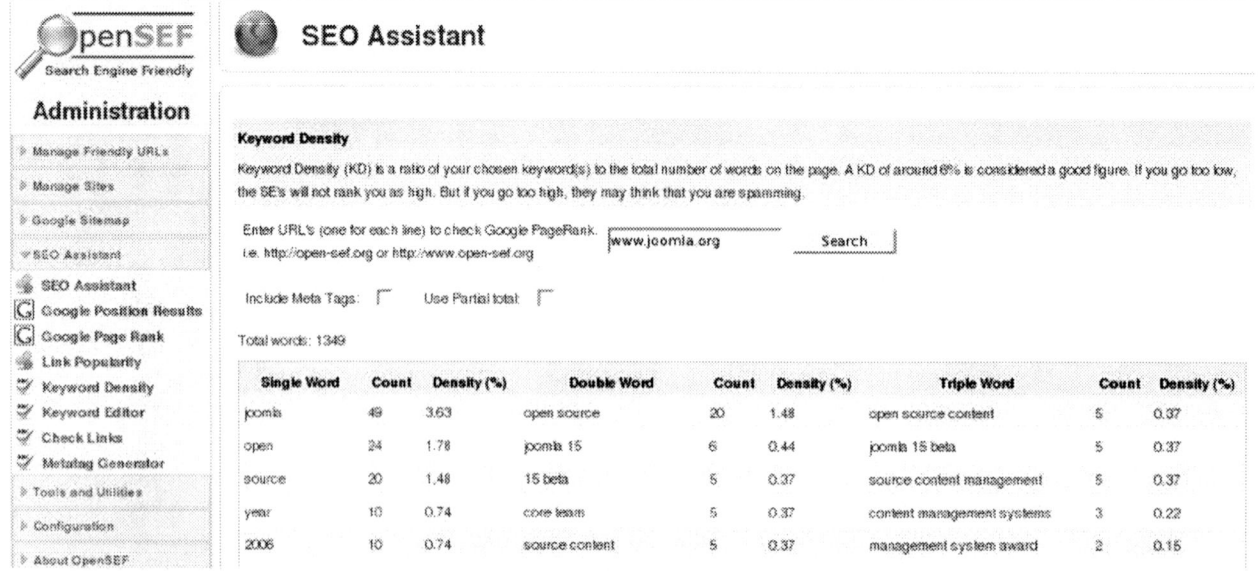

Screenshot of an OpenSEF Keyword Density analysis of http://www.joomla.org/

OpenSEF can also generate a Google Sitemap, work across multiple websites, and even allow the administrator to specify the text for the search engine friendly URLs. OpenSEF can also replace the links to various components with friendly URL's. These can be explicitly configured. Be sure to click the Save button to save your configuration changes.

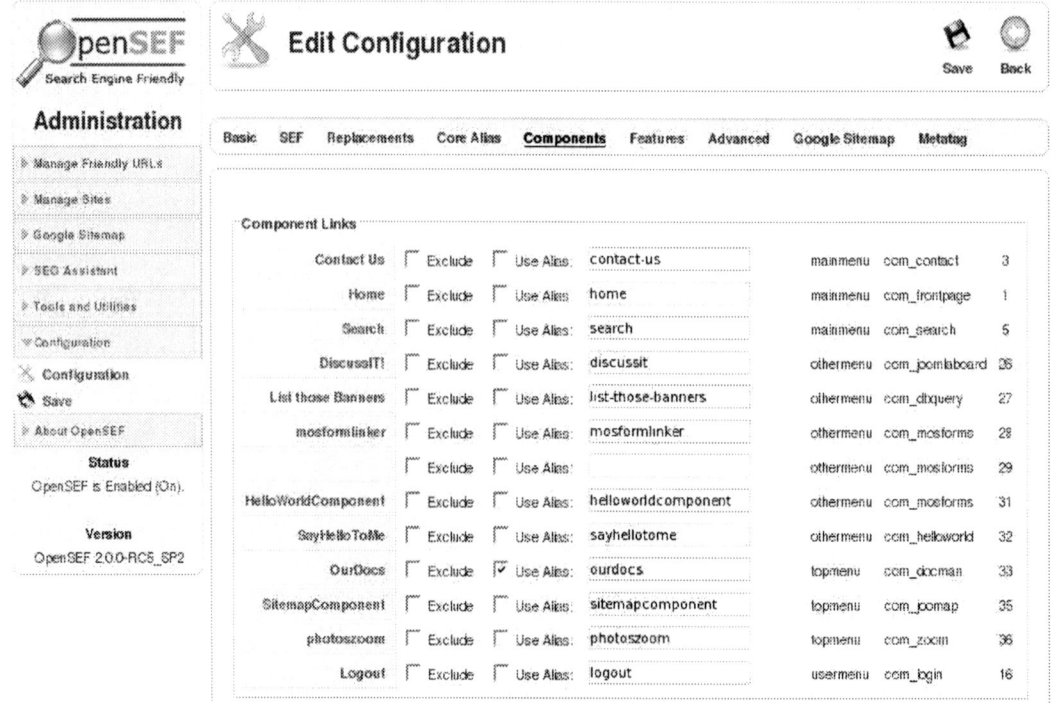

Discussion Forum

Joomlaboard Forum Component

http://extensions.joomla.org/component/option,com_mtree/task,viewlink/link_id,133/Itemid,35/

Joomlaboard provides a discussion forum to Joomla!. Simply install it and use it. Joomlaboard was formerly known as Simpleboard. The installation process is to download the latest file and then install it with the Administration tool just as with any component. Then clicking the link to "Install Sample Data" gives you a pre-configured board and takes you to the nice control panel for Joomlaboard.

Screenshot of Joomlaboard's control panel.

The configuration for Joomlaboard is very complete. Not only can the Basics like the Title be setup easily but also the workings such as the threads per page, size of text entry areas, and much more. Joomlaboard may be configured to allow anyone access to the board, or to allow only registered users to post messages, or to allow only registered users access to the board. Probably you'll want to click the "Joomla Configuration" button and then the Security tab and change the "Public Read/Write" to be more restrictive. Note it can work with the Badwords component to filter posts with Badwords; but, in reality, spam filtering on message boards has become a new science and some contribution needs to be made in this area.

The final product is a clean and very functional message board. Man, life is easy with Joomla!

Support HelpDesk

WebAmoeba Ticket System

http://www.webamoeba.co.uk/joomla/

The WebAmoeba Ticket System (WATS) component adds a support request and response system. WATS provides a way to submit, respond to, and resolve support requests (tickets). The tickets can be marked as open, closed or dead. The system requires a login to Joomla to submit new tickets, so the requests themselves cannot be entered unless customers have a login to the Joomla installation.

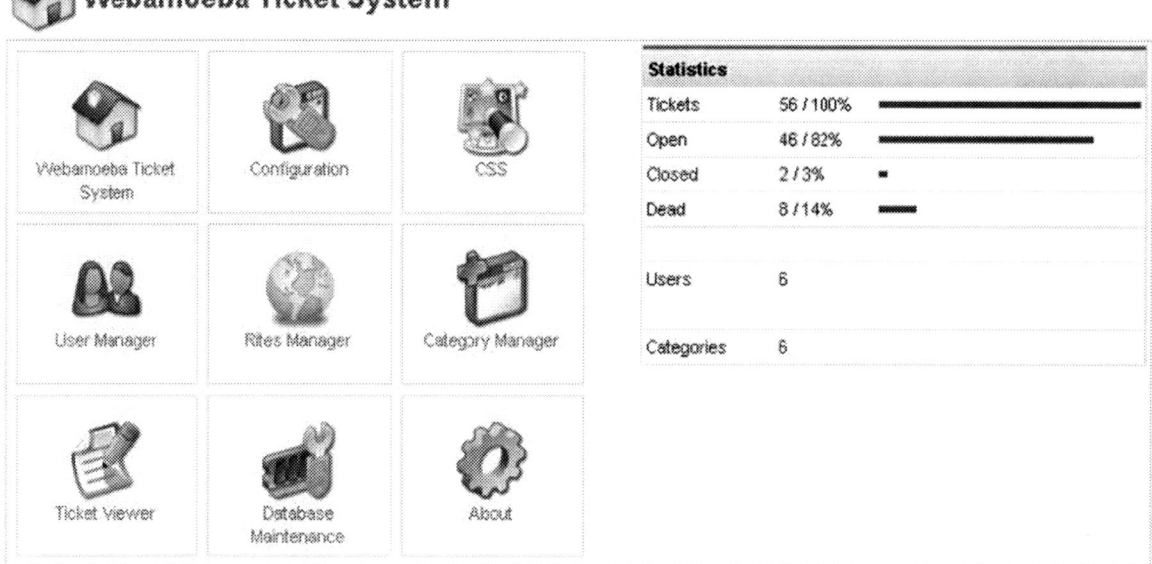

The Webamoeba Ticket System's Control Panel.

WATS has a fully customizable category and user rights facility. It supports 11 different languages, to which more can be easily added. Unlike its rivals it has an intelligent upgrade system. Additional features such as custom fields, status, and an FAQ are all planned for the future.

WATS was the first helpdesk open source project to be released for Joomla! and Mambo. It was setup in response to the commercial alternative 'GLOBODIGITAL Support Centre Helpdesk'. Two other opensource alternatives are available for Joomla! and Mambo, a6 helpdesk and JoomlaDesk. a6 helpdesk is no longer in development, but the last version (released in 2004) is still available. JoomlaDesk but is still in the beta phase of development so not yet ready for evaluation. Clearly additional features such as a severity rate and other states such as "investigating" or "working" may be added to the support request tracking packages. Integration with a project management application such as dotproject or project management components within Joomla! could be beneficial as well.

Username: tu1
Group: administrator
Organisation: individual

New Ticket	Support Categories	Ticket Number
Submit a new ticket	Help Desk	WATS- [ ] Go

Default Category
If there are no suiatble categories submit your tickets here ;)

Ticket Name	Posts	Last Post
fghfg tu1: 9-Sep-2006	17	9-Sep-2006 (05:29)
sdfsdf tu1: 26-Aug-2006	3	26-Aug-2006 (03:12)
sdfsdf tu1: 26-Aug-2006	1	26-Aug-2006 (01:50)
sdfsdf tu1: 26-Aug-2006	1	26-Aug-2006 (01:50)
asdasd tu1: 26-Aug-2006	4	26-Aug-2006 (01:40)

Pages: 1 ≥ (All, Personal, Open, Closed, Dead)

Users
Manage Users

Username	Organisation	Group	Email
tu3 (test user 3)	individual	advisor	tu3@webamoeba.co.uk
tu4 (test user 4)	individual	advisor	jg8949@aol.com
tu1 (test user 1)	individual	administrator	tu1@webamoeba.co.uk

Add User

WebAmoeba Ticket System for Mambo and Joomla

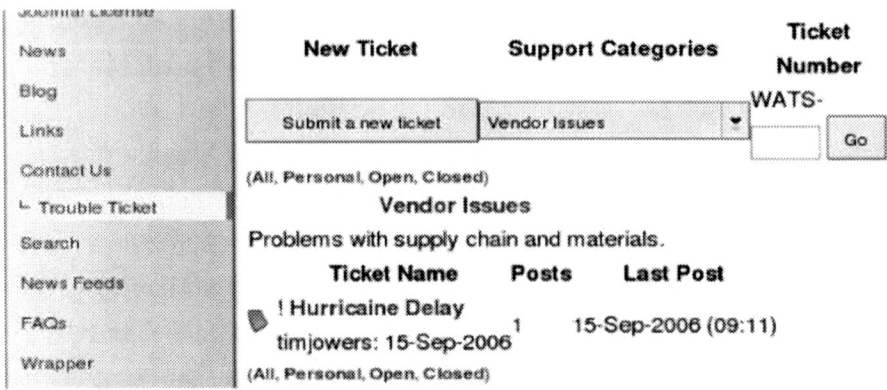

Screenshot of support requests/tickets in the WebAmoeba Ticket System.

Coding a Component

You can read through the Joomla! source code and modify it to fit your needs; but the best way to integrate is by writing a component because with a component you can simply upgrade to a new release of Joomla! and not have to rewrite your code. You can learn exactly how a component works since the Joomla! source code is given to you. You can even read through the code of existing components.

Hello Joomla!

The simplest component will display a message to a web page in the Administrator area. The message will be "Hello Joomla!". First we will add the component to the Administrator area. To do this we will create two files within /var/www/html/bizapps/joomla/administrator/.

1. First create a new subdirectory named com_helloworld within /var/www/html/bizapps/joomla/administrator/components. Note the magically delicious way the directory name "com_helloworld" will match the name of the component. That's the magic that makes it all work. Here's the science behind the magic. The web address we will use for testing is:

    http://localhost/bizapps/joomla/administrator/index2.php?option=com_helloworld

And if we look in administrator/index2.php at line 32 we will see where the option request parameter is retrieved:

```
32    $option = strval( strtolower( mosGetParam( $_REQUEST, 'option', '' ) ) );
```

index2.php uses the mosMainFrame class; so, eventually down around line 1267 in the _setAdminPaths of the file includes/joomla.php one finds where the parameter value "com_helloworld" is parsed to read out the "helloworld" string and then this string is used to build the filenames which the Administrator will call. The essential lines are:

```
1267    $prefix = substr( $option, 0, 4 );
```

and

```
1286    $this->_path->admin =
            "$basePath/administrator/components/$option/admin.$name.php";
```

2. So we need one file named admin.helloworld.php within com_hello. This file provides the functions called by the Joomla! Administrator.

3. The second file will be named helloworld.html. This file is referenced by admin.helloworld.php to create the actual web page to be displayed.

Coding a Component

So, let's look at the files. First of all let's look at the helloworld.html file. It is quite simple:

```
<h1>Hello Joomla!<h1>
```

Really, that's it. Remember the HTML will be embedded within a larger page so we should not specify <html>, <head>, or <body> tags; so the HTML is simple.

Next let's look at the admin.helloworld.php file which defines the component to Joomla!. It simply defines the function Joomla! should call when displaying this component.

```
<?php
/**
* @version 0.1
* @package HelloWorld
* @copyright CopyLeft
* @license http://www.gnu.org/copyleft/gpl.html GNU/GPL
*/
// Do not allow a script kiddie to call this directly.
defined( '_VALID_MOS' ) or header("Location: /");
require_once($mosConfig_absolute_path .'/includes/patTemplate/patTemplate.php');
    $tmpl =& patFactory::createTemplate( $option, true, false);
    $tmpl->setRoot( dirname( __FILE__ ) . '/' );
    $tmpl->setAttribute( 'body', 'src', 'helloworld.html' );
    $tmpl->displayParsedTemplate( 'form' );
?>
```
Listing of admin.helloworld.php.

OK, almost done. You should have created the two files are in the com_helloworld subdirectory of /var/www/html/bizapps/joomla/administrator/components. Let's test it. Enter the URL into the web browser:

http://localhost/bizapps/joomla/administrator/index2.php?option=com_helloworld

Now you should see the message "Hello Joomla!" in the web browser. If not then see the debugging section below.

Here is a play by play description of the admin.helloworld.php file. The first line

```
defined( '_VALID_MOS' ) or header("Location: /");
```

114

Coding a Component

checks to see if our PHP file is being called from within Joomla or if someone is trying to crack into the site by calling it directly. Try to call it directly and see what happens. Try the address:

http://localhost/bizapps/joomla/administrator/components/com_helloworld/admin.helloworld.php

Some programmers prefer to use "`or die('Bad access');`" as the last part of the conditional check. That's OK too.

The next major line includes `patTemplate.php` and that provides the magic to add our form onto the page. Let's don't be shy: open up `includes/patTemplate/patTemplate.php` and see what the `patFactory::createTemplate` method does. It creates the data structure to represent this part of the web page – or pulls the structure from cache. `SetRoot` instructs Joomla! where to look for the HTML file and `setAttribute` specifies the HTML file's name. By using patTemplate's patFactory we are taking advantage of the Joomla! infrastructure. One of the built-in, standard templates provided is called "form", and that's what the last line uses.

Debugging

The first step is to read through your code for obvious errors. Next check the error log for errors such as typing errors. I normally have a terminal window running with a tail on the Apache log such as with "tail -f /var/log/httpd/error_log". The "-f" means any new messages will be written to the screen.

One may find one's Joomla! setup in la-la land and find the following message when ones attempts to access the website:

Jowers Genealogy Website

**This site is temporarily unavailable.
Please notify the System Administrator**

Screenshot of the error message on a Joomla! Website.

One may be quite miffed as to what happened. A quick look into the error_log reveals nothing. Hmm. Check the obvious.

1. Is Apache up? Yes, clearly it is since the page loaded.
2. Is the mysql service/daemon running?

   In this case, indeed the database was down. How easy to fix. Just start the mysql daemon/service.
3. What messages are in the error_log?
4. At the worst, rollback the website files and/or database to a past configuration which was backed up earlier.

Hello World

In the HelloJoomla example we made a Component appear in the Administrator area; now we focus on a complete component to display on the main website. Several more files will be needed. The important tasks are:

1. Create a file to handle the front end and render the web page HTML for the web visitors.
   1. helloworld.php
2. Create the files to show in the Administrator for the component. We did the most basic case of this above. This will be launched from the Component menu in the Administrator area. This file will now also handle the Administrator buttons of New, Publish, Unpublish, Delete, Edit, Save, and Cancel in Joomla! This will be launched when someone has selected the component already and then clicks one of the buttons or the link to an existing listing entry of an instance of the

Coding a Component

component.
   1. admin.helloworld.php
   2. helloworld.html
3. Create the installation files.
   1. install.helloworld.php
   2. uninstall.helloworld.php
   3. helloworld.xml
      1. the XML file controls the install. It contains the component's name, file names, and queries to install and uninstall the component.

Step by Step

helloworld.php

```
<?php
/**
* @package HelloWorld
* @version 1.0
* @copyright CopyLeft
* @license http://www.gnu.org/copyleft/gpl.html GNU/GPL
*/
defined( '_VALID_MOS' ) or die('Bad access');
?>

<h2>Hello World from a complete Component</h2>
```

The frontend file is simple. It declares some source annotated comments, checks for valid access from within Joomla!, and then simply shows some HTML. In a real-world implementation one would put their PHP code here and check the $task variable and/or others passed by the menu.

admin.helloworld.php and **helloworld.htm** are the same as before.

install.helloworld.php and **uninstall.helloworld.php** are straightforward for us. These give us an opportunity to execute PHP code if needed.

Coding a Component

```php
<?php
function com_install() {
    echo 'Woohoo! Hello World installation underway';
    return 'Hello World is now installed';
}
?>
```
install.helloworld.php

```php
<?php
function com_uninstall() {
    echo 'Goodbye! Hello World uninstallation underway';
    return 'Hello World is now removed.';
}
?>
```
uninstall.helloworld.php

helloworld.xml
```xml
<?xml version="1.0" ?>
<mosinstall type="component">
 <name>helloworld</name>
 <creationDate>12/12/2006</creationDate>
 <author>Max Weber</author>
 <copyright>CopyLeft</copyright>
 <authorUrl>www.serviza.comt</authorUrl>
 <version>1.0</version>
 <files>
  <filename>helloworld.php</filename>
 </files>
 <installfile>
  <filename>install.helloworld.php</filename>
 </installfile>
 <uninstallfile>
  <filename>uninstall.helloworld.php</filename>
 </uninstallfile>
    <administration>
     <menu>helloworld</menu>
     <files>
        <filename>admin.helloworld.php</filename>
        <filename>helloworld.html</filename>
     </files>
    </administration>
</mosinstall>
```

The XML installation file can have queries and much more but the simplest install file only specifies

Coding a Component

the author's information and the files to install.

Zip It

Zip it to install it. Actually you can tar.gz it or whatever as well. Once the zip file is made then the installation is the same as any other Component: simply use the menu Installers->Components, browse for the file, and then click the button to "Upload File & Install". The final step is to test it out like any component such as adding a menu option for a New Component using the Menu->othermenu choice. The component now functions within the Administrator area and also in the actual web page. Whereas we could not add PHP code to a Content Item, we can now execute PHP code in response to requests on the website and have done so in a maintainable and upgradeable component which we could even redistribute to others.

Admin Toolbar

As our component grows in capabilities we'll want to support the buttons for administering it; so create a file to control what buttons are shown in the Administrator area for the component. This is fairly boilerplate for all components.

4. toolbar.helloworld.php

```php
<?php
/**
* @package HelloWorld
* @version 1.0
* @copyright CopyLeft
* @license http://www.gnu.org/copyleft/gpl.html GNU/GPL, see
LICENSE.php
*/

defined( '_VALID_MOS' ) or die('Bad access');

switch( $task )
{
   case "new":  // add a new instance or configuration
   case "edit": // edit an instance or configuration
       mosMenuBar::startTable();
       mosMenuBar::save();
       mosMenuBar::cancel();
       mosMenuBar::endTable();
     break;
   default: // when the component is selected from the menu
```

Coding a Component

```
            mosMenuBar::startTable();
            mosMenuBar::publishList();
            mosMenuBar::unpublishList();
        mosMenuBar::spacer();
        mosMenuBar::spacer();
            mosMenuBar::addNew();
            mosMenuBar::editList();
            mosMenuBar::deleteList();
            mosMenuBar::endTable();
        break;
}

?>
```

Don't forget to update the install XML with a new <file> element to specify this file is to be installed; or better yet, read the next section and implement this as two files and use PHP classes. You can also simply drop this in the administrator/components/com_helloworld directory for testing purposes. Remember the "magic" of the component name and the files the Joomla! Administrator looks for? If you look into the file includes/joomla.php you will see how the toolbar filename is searched using the exact same logic – line 1291 to be exact.

PHP Classes

Up until now the Keep It Simple Stupid rule has ruled. As code complexity grows so must organization be introduced; and classes are one great way to group together functionality and make clear what is being done within the program. Without classes we would have a flat space of 100, 200, or more functions or have to really filter through which files were referenced from which others (via the PHP require_once keyword for instance). As an example, let's rework the toolbar code above but use classes. A new class is introduced in a new file named toolbar.helloworld.html.php.

```
<?php
defined( '_VALID_MOS' ) or die('Bad access');

class menuSpec
{
    function ShowInstanceMenus() {
        mosMenuBar::startTable();
        mosMenuBar::save();
        mosMenuBar::cancel();
        mosMenuBar::endTable();
    }
    function ShowDefaultMenus() {
        mosMenuBar::startTable();
```

Coding a Component

```
            mosMenuBar::publishList();
            mosMenuBar::unpublishList();
        mosMenuBar::spacer();
        mosMenuBar::spacer();
            mosMenuBar::addNew();
            mosMenuBar::editList();
            mosMenuBar::deleteList();
            mosMenuBar::endTable();
        }
    }
?>
```

toolbar.helloworld.html.php

This new file refactors the code from toolbar.helloworld.php. Using classes to organize code is called "Object Oriented Programming"; and OO purists love refactoring because it results in simple, manageable classes and because maybe someday the code can be reused. For instance, maybe a default toolbar.default.html.php class will be added to Joomla! so Components can simply use it and get the default arrangement of buttons. PHP gives a sort of deja-vu to former C++ programmers because of the same syntax for the class keyword, the statement delimiters of {, the class::function delimiters, and the case statements. Thank goodness no ; is required after the ending } for the class definition!

We now need to update the original toolbar.helloworld.php file since much of its code has been factored out.

```
<?php
defined( '_VALID_MOS' ) or die('Bad access');

require_once( $mainframe->getPath( 'toolbar_html' ) );

switch( $task )
{
   case "new":  // add a new instance or configuration
   case "edit": // edit an instance or configuration
        menuSpec::ShowInstanceMenus();
      break;
   default: // when the component is selected from the menu
        menuSpec::ShowDefaultMenus();
      break;
}
?>
```

Notice the case statement code has been updated to call the functions in the newly defined class. But how does the PHP interpreter know what file defines the class? The require_once keyword in PHP tells

PHP to include the file. A funkadelic helper method from Joomla! called "getPath" identifies the actual file. The funkiness is "getPath" parses out the _ in `toolbar_html` and replaces it with `.helloworld.` which is made from the name of the Component. Go check out line 1327 of the getPath function in includes/joomla.php to see the funky magic.

Securing a Component

Of course each component should be only accessible by the appropriate users. For instance, only an administrator should be able to configure the component in the Administrator area. E.g.

```
// ensure user has access to this function
if (!($acl->acl_check( 'administration', 'edit', 'users', $my-
>usertype, 'components', 'all' )| $acl->acl_check( 'administration',
'edit', 'users', $my->usertype, 'components', 'com_banners' ))) {
    mosRedirect( 'index2.php', _NOT_AUTH );
}
```

TTS Component Example

The Java FreeTTS and the Festival FLOSS projects make Text-To-Speech available to anyone for the low reasonable price of free; so, let's accept the gift and use it within Joomla!. Let's make a component to read out the news items. It will use the text2wave program of festival and create an audio file from the items in the jos_content table. Submit your solutions to CourseProjectOSPJoomla@Serviza.com.

References

Many other references will help you master writing components.
- Andrew Eddie's "Hello World" tutorial uses a PHP class, comments, and a few other aspects of Joomla!.
    http://help.joomla.org/content/view/773/125/
- Open Source Matters' "Hello World" tutorial builds on Andrew Eddie's tutorial and allows tabs and data passing in the Administrator area.
    http://help.joomla.org/content/view/774/125/
- A complete tutorial for creating a Component for Mambo which also applies to Joomla! 1.0.x.
    http://devbay.com/content/view/15/43/
- Joseph LeBlanc's Mambo tutorials which also work for Joomla!.
    www.jlleblanc.com/joomla/Tutorials/The_Daily_Message_Joomla_Component_Tutorial/
    http://www.jlleblanc.com/content/view/12/54 (using tabs in the Admin area)

www.jlleblanc.com/joomla/Tutorials/Daily_Message_with_HTML_editors_%26_Dates/
(integrating the Joomla! WYSIWIG editor and Joomla! calendar into your component)
- Another Mambo example to create a component with a front end and Admin area:
  http://www.mambohut.com/content/view/158/58/
- Creating an Upgradeable Mambo Component
  http://www.lummie.co.uk/content/category/4/16/58/

Templates

Joomla! 1.x laid out pages using an PHP infrastructure mechanism called patTemplate. Joomla! 1.5 has moved to using Smarty templates which is a standard for many PHP-based applications. patTemplate is still supported but not recommended due to performance and deprecation. The big idea for templates in PHP is one can get whip-lash trying to decipher PHP code embedded within HTML code; the confusion is especially bad when the PHP is generating HTML such as table rows for listing on a web page. Sadly this is an unsolved problem and has been attacked for years in almost all web layers: ASP, JSP, PHP, and you-name-it. In an ideal world the code can be separated from the presentation but in a real world the presentation has to be dynamic and customized therefore integrating code is the only solution. In at least one author's opinion, the attempt to take the coding out of websites is just plain futile. Now that the grump has ranted, let's see what Templates are in Joomla!.

In Joomla! the content, or articles, are already well separated from the page layout. The Template defines the layout, the colors, and other appearance and will be applied to the text presented by the articles, modules, and components. The articles and content are not affected even if the Template is changed altogether. The major aspects managed by a Template are:

1) Menus
2) Articles
3) Advertisements
4) Modules
5) Components
6) Graphics and other Appearance

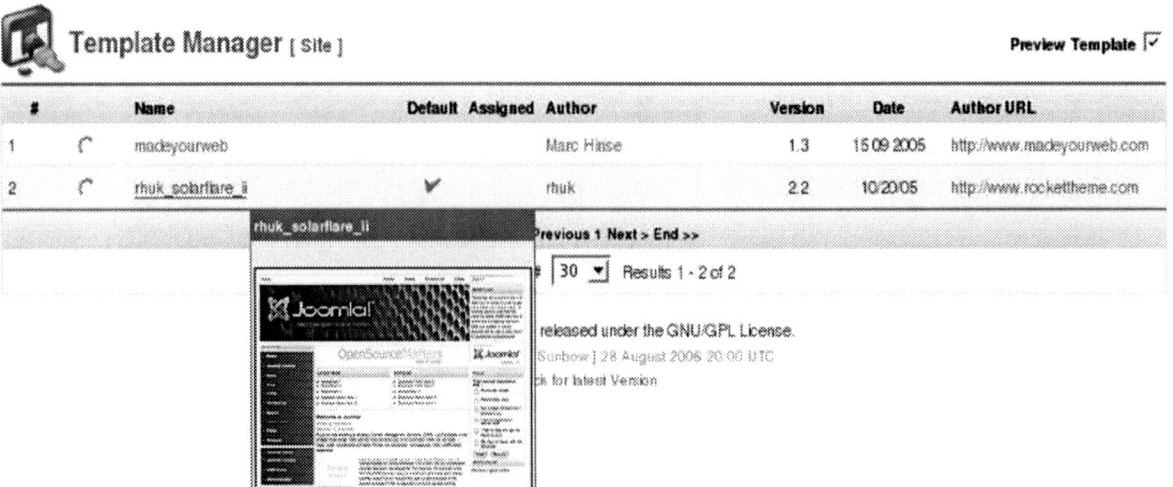

Screenshot showing Template choices for Joomla! 1.0.

For instance, the Template determines the number of and placement of menus. The default installation in Joomla! 1.0 has four menus and the default installation in Joomla! 1.5 has six menus.

Screenshot showing a default Template for Joomla! 1.5.

Edit CSS

One can simply and easily edit the Cascading Style Sheet, or CSS, for a Template by selecting the radio button beside the template and clicking the "Edit CSS" button. (In 1.5 one must first click the "Edit" button). A CSS is a very centrally located place to change the colors, borders, and other web page appearance items. It may even be used to control rollovers where the text changes color or size when the mouse moves over it. Corporate colors and look can be quickly updated because Joomla! makes CSS editing so simple.

Edit HTML

Editing the main HTML for the Template is not so simple. Many corporations have strict web user interface guidelines and the simple fact that so much can be shown and navigated through with menus in Joomla! may conflict with those guidelines. The Template HTML is the place to get busy with drastic changes to the layout of pages in Joomla!. As one can see these make use of including other files for processing the PHP for menus, modules, blogs, tables, and such. In 1.0 one will see functions like mosShowHead() and mosLoadModules() whereas in 1.5 one will see repeated uses of jdoc:include. Keywords stored with the module in the database control the module location on the web page; that is, *top*, *left*, *right*, or *bottom*.

Final Notes

Moving the Whole Shebang

Moving a Joomla! website is possible and not too difficult.

Migrate MySQL

Joomla! is a database driven system so clearly the first task is to copy the database if a different database installation will be used. MySQL has several ways of doing this. One way is to use the MySQL Administrator and to Backup the database from one server and then restore it to another. The low tech command line way is to export the database and then import it into the new database.

```
mysqldump bizapps_joomla > backupdb.dmp
```

Copy the backupdb.dmp file to a CD or otherwise transfer it to the destination system. On the destination system create the new database and fill it up with data. The database name can be different; and if so you'll want to change it in the configuration.php file in the joomla directory.

```
mysql
mysql> create database bizapps_joomla;
mysql> quit
mysql bizapps_joomla < backupdb.dmp
```

Note that Mysql also supports mirroring so a hot standby can easily be made and will have all of the data of the main system. If the main system goes down, no problem. Just update the IP for the domain or have the load balancer start sending requests to the hot standby.

Migrate Joomla! Files

Migrating Joomla! files is quite easy. Simply archive the folder or otherwise copy it to the new destination. Then be sure to set the owner back to apache if needed. For instance, with the rsync command one can easily transfer a directory from one machine to another while retaining permissions.

```
rsync -avz /var/www/html/bizapps/joomla 192.168.0.32:/var/www/html/joomla
```

As mentioned before, edit configuration.php if the configuration parameters such as the destination directory, the database name, the database login, or URL are different in the new scheme.

Joomla! Consultants

Numerous Joomla web resources, consultancies, and other sources of help and information can be found with a quick Internet search. The rates are in-line with support for other software products[17].

---

17 See, for instance, https://www.phil-taylor.com/fees/

Index

Administration 9, 10, 99
Apache 19, 24, 28
Article .... 13, 15 (defined), 33, 52
Backup 42, 127
Banner 35, 37, 38
Blog 16
Category 15, 50, 94
Check-in .... see Version Control
Component 17, 78, 113
Contact Us 34, 39, 79
Content Management System 9
Control Panel ...... see Administration
CSS .... see Style and Layout
Database 57, 87
Debugging .... see Troubleshooting
Design 52
Discussion Forum 109
Document Management 93
Domain Name 29, 35, 130
eCommerce 97
FAQ 34
Flash 38
Front Page 50
Forms 81
Global Configuration 32
Google Adsense 38, 76
Helpdesk 111
htaccess 104
Installation 19, 25, 117
Item .... 12, See Article

Joomla! 1.5 versus 1.0 .... 11, 15, 16,
.... 52, 53, 55, 69, 73, 74, 126
Layout 57, 124
Legacy Mode 74
Link 16
Mambot 17
Mass Mail 39
Media Manager 40
Menu 11, 15, 34
Module 17, 70
MySQL 20, 28, 68, 69, 116, 127, 131
Newsfeed 39
Password 29
PHP 22, 59-69
Polls 41
Programming Joomla! 52, 71, 113
Search Engine 36, 47, 104-108
Section 15, 50
Security 43, 58
Statistics 90
Style 57, 125
Syndicate 39
Table 16
Template 124
Troubleshooting: 20, 27, 64, 73, 95, 107, 115
Users 18
Version Control 18
Web Link 34, 40
Workflow 95

Appendix A: How-To Setup a Domain Name in Apache

1. Decide on a domain name. The example here will be: gr8pl8es.com
2. Normally one would rent the domain name be paying a Domain Registrar. Then the Domain Name would be mapped to an Internet Address. This can be handled by a network administrator.
3. Edit /etc/hosts and enter the domain name and the local, or loopback, IP address which is 127.0.0.1. For example, enter:

```
127.0.0.1       gr8pl8es.com
```

1. Validate the domain may be navigated to in the web browser (you'll have to restart the web browser if it is already running as it probably caches DNS lookups):

```
http://gr8pla8es.com/
```

1. Configure a subfolder for this domain's web pages.
   1. Create a directory such as /gr8pl8 in /var/www/html

```
II. cd /var/www/html
III. mkdir gr8pla8s
IV. cd gr8pla8s
```

1. Copy the helloworld.html file into that folder but with the name of index.html.

```
V. cp ../helloworld.html index.html
```

1. Change this index.html to contain the domain name or another unique message.

```
VI. gedit index.html
```

1. Update the new file and the new directory so the user apache can access them. The Apache web server runs as apache so needs permission to access the files. "-R" recurses into the folder and also change files within the folder.

```
VII. cd /var/www/html
VIII. chown apache:apache -R   gr8pla8s
```

1. Setup Apache to send web page requests for the domain to start in the new folder. The "DocumentRoot" identifies the folder to Apache.

```
IX. gedit /etc/httpd/conf/httpd.conf
```

1. Enter the following declaration at the end of the file. Be sure to use the domain name you chose if it is not gr8pla8s.com.

```
# Virtual host gr8pl8es.com
<VirtualHost www.gr8pl8es.com>
        DocumentRoot /var/www/html/gr8pl8s
        ServerAdmin webmaster@gr8pl8es.com
        ServerName www.gr8pl8es.com
        ServerSignature email
        DirectoryIndex index.html index.htm
</VirtualHost>
```

Appendix A: How-To Setup a Domain Name in Apache

1. Save the file and close it.
2. Restart the Apache web server so it will enable this domain.
   1. CLI: `service httpd restart`
   2. GUI: Applications->System Settings->Server Settings->Services. Click on httpd and click restart.
3. Validate the domain may be navigated to in the web browser and the HTML file is retrieved from the new folder: http://gr8pla8es.com/

1. In order to navigate to use "www" to http://www.gr8pla8es.com then www.gr8pl8es.com should also be added to the /etc/hosts file.

Appendix B: MySQL Database Backups

Database backups are vitally important and must be performed on a regular basis. Database mirroring, or replication, can reduce the risk of data loss; however, database backups can ensure an uncorrupted database copy has been made and is available for reference in the future.

1. Backup mysql[18]
   1. The simplest way to backup mysql is to stop the mysql service and make a backup copy of all of the databases as follows.
      1. service mysqld stop
      2. Copy the data.
         1. Simply copy all of the table files such as (*.frm, *.MYD, and *.MYI files).
         2. Or use the sqldump command of Mysql. Specify a database name to backup one database or no name to backup all databases.
            1. mysqldump --tab=/path/to/some/dir --opt db_name
      3. Restore the data
         1. Copy the files over the database file.
         2. Or use the mysql program:
            1. mysql db_name < backupfile.sql
   2. Backups may also be performed while the system is running.

---

18 Refer to http://dev.mysql.com/doc/refman/5.0/en/backup.html for more documentation.

Appendix B: MySQL Database Backups

1. Open a terminal.
2. Create a directory for backups.
   1. mkdir backup
   2. cd backup
   3. mysqldump –all-databases > alldbs.dmp
3. Change the database.
   1. mysql
   2. show databases;
   3. use bizapps_WebCalendar;
   4. Bring up a web browser to http://localhost/bizapps/WebCalendar/
   5. Add an entry if none is listed by using the steps in the Business Management and Operations chapter on the Shared Calendar.
   6. In mysql, enter the following commands.
      1. show tables;
      2. select * from webcal_entry;
      3. Delete the displayed entry.
         1. Determine the id of the entry and use it in the delete SQL clause: e.g. 2.
         2. delete from webcal_entry where cal_id=2;
         3. quit
   7. Redisplay the web page and determine the entry is no longer present.
   8. Restore the mysql database;
      1. In a terminal in the backup folder enter the following:
      2. mysql < alldumps
      3. Verify the data is restored by refreshing the web page.
      4. One can also run mysql and use the database to select the table and see the data is restored.
   4. mysqlhotcopy may also be used for backups while the mysqld MySQL RDBMS is running.
3. Incremental backups save only data added since the last backup.
   1. Configure mysqld to start with the –log-bin option.
   2. MySQL creates the bin log files automatically.
   3. Restore from a mysqldump and then apply the latest bin log file such as mysqlbinlog binlog.9 | mysql.

Printed in the United States
74603LV00009B/53